Attacking Football's Wing-T

KENNY RATLEDGE

Harding Press
Haworth, NJ 07641

Library of Congress Cataloging-in-Publication Data

Ratledge, Kenny.
Attacking football's Wing-T / Kenny Ratledge.
p. cm.
ISBN 1-890450-06-5 (pbk.)
1. Football—Defense. 2. Football—Coaching. I. Title.

GV951.18.R28 2000
796.332′2—dc21

00-044895

ISBN 1-890450-06-5

Printed in the United States of America

HARDING PRESS
P.O. Box 141
Haworth, NJ 07641
hardingpress@earthlink.net
www.hardingpress.com

Books by and for the coaching profession

I would like to dedicate this book to my wife, Debbie,
and my two children, Patrick and Laura.
Without their support I would not be able to do what I enjoy and that is to coach football. Four to five months a year I am in and out of their lives. Debbie is left to be both a father and mother to the kids. I truly appreciate her efforts.
I hope they understand.

Acknowledgments

I would like to thank the coaches at Sevier County High School who have helped in the development and implementation of the plan. I would like to thank them for their valuable input. Thanks go to Bryan Atchley and Toby Ward, our defensive line coaches. Thanks to Billy Ward, the secondary coach, who helped define our secondary play. Todd Loveday is an asset as the safeties coach. Tony Linginfelter, our offensive coordinator, has given us insights on the wing. Tony had exposure to the wing at a previous stop. I would also include Chuck Field who, along with myself, coaches the linebackers. Thanks to our freshman coaches, Dan Deremer and Kevin Hurst, for teaching the plan to our freshmen. Thanks also to David Youell, our trainer, who keeps our players physically able to implement the plan. Gratitude is also extended to middle school coaches Allen Robbins and Steve Helton.

Thanks go to Gary Roach, our principal, and Al Cardiel, the athletic director, for allowing me to work at the best job I have ever had.

I would give special thanks to Steve Brewer who gives his coaches a job to do and allows them the freedom to do it.

My appreciation also goes to Dixon Brown, our computer expert, for his help in preparing the manuscript. And a very special thank you to Darlene Rosenthal for typing the manuscript. Without Darlene, Sevier County High School could not function.

These acknowledgments would not be complete without a special remembrance of our beloved team chaplain, the late Reverend David Walker – our twelfth man – who led and inspired us with his belief in

"Faith, fight, finish." *(II Timothy 4:7)*

We miss you.

Contents

How This Book Will Help You

The scheme presented here will make it easy to adjust to the wheels and movements that the Wing-T throws at your defense. It will give defenders well-defined keys that will cut down on any hesitancy. It will give defenders reads they can believe in so they do not get frustrated trying to find the ball. Option responsibilities are easily defined and understood.

This scheme will enable your defense to get quick linebacker support on sweeps. In many cases the linebacker will get to the frontside guard before the guard can turn upfield. For years coaches have preached two schools of thought on how to defend the Wing-T. One school says penetration is the key, and the other school advises sit and read. This scheme uses parts of both philosophies.

The scheme illustrated here will allow your defense to have six men on the 20 series down trap. If read correctly, the defense can combat the counter criss cross with five men. When the offense runs the red trap, they are running at one or two unblocked defenders. We played one game where, on the third red trap the offense ran, the fullback took the handoff and tried to run to the sideline. He knew, if his coach didn't, that the play was dead in the water. On one play in 1997, we had all 11 defenders on the tackle on the red isolation.

The pass defense presented here will allow your defense to get body on body with all eligible pass receivers on each play. There are no seams or dead areas for the offense to attack. The defense versus the red waggle will get a quick pull up on the QB with an unblocked linebacker on a free run at the QB. On the same red waggle, we get a double team on the tailback and a possible double on the tight end.

The 20 series waggle is also pulled up quickly, along with a double team on the tight end and fullback. This system presents a simple but flexible linebacker pass-coverage scheme in which linebackers can be used to double receivers or can be used as run-through players to attack a good running QB.

You may choose to use all the defensive concepts presented here, or you may decide to pick and choose. Either way, we feel that these concepts will help any coach's ability to attack and stop the Wing-T. This material is presented with the understanding that the contents apply to attacking the Wing-T offense and not to a team that runs some Wing-T plays along with another type of offense. Let it be understood also that the Wing-T described here is what we see in our part of the country. One last note to Wing-T aficionados: The author has the chalk last.

1

Background of the Defense

The defensive scheme presented in this book is derived from a multiple 4-3 front with quarters (four-across) coverage. See Diagram 1-1.

We are an attack and read-on-the-run defense. We, like everyone else, are trying to get as much speed on the field as we can. We will move marginal safeties to linebackers, down-the-line linebackers to ends, and ends to tackle.

As a general rule, we do not flip-flop the front, but on occasion we will flip-flop personnel to take advantage of mismatches.

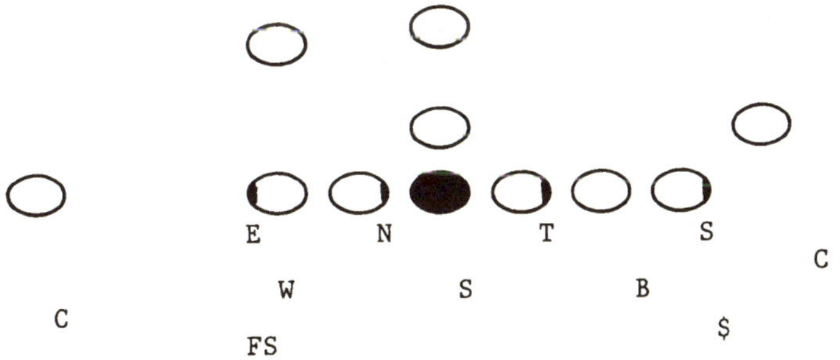

DIAGRAM 1-1
Base Defense

TACKLES

Recently we have not been blessed with a lot of size at this position. Our tackles are of average size but are fairly quick. This suits our philosophy just fine because we would never choose bulk over speed anyway. There are things in our scheme that we can do to cover up any size differential. We spend a lot of practice time with our tackles on takeoff drills. We want to crowd the ball and come off on the snap. We tell our linemen that we want to beat the offense to the punch. We want to get there an inch before they do. We want to be fundamentally sound with the use of our hands. We have a progression we go through to perfect the use of our hands. We base out of a 4-3 structure, but we are very multiple with our fronts. We want to present recognition and blocking problems by aligning in various shades, jumping gaps and seams, slanting from head up or shades, and running opposites. We use a run-first, read-second philosophy with the line. We feel that the way we practice our linemen allows them to align in various shades or gaps and be successful. We package our reads with an inside or outside shade designation. We teach linemen the fundamental reads from a basic outside shade, which includes a 1, 3, 5, or 9 shade. This allows the lineman to play on an outside shade on any of the offensive linemen. In turn we also teach them to play from an inside shade, which we term a 2, 4, or 7 alignment. This allows the lineman to function in an inside shade on any of the offensive linemen. Instead of coaching a player to be a tackle, nose, or end, which may limit his ability to play another position, or teaching him to play as a right tackle or left end, we use the inside/outside designation, which will allow him to play more than one position or to play on the right or left side of the defense.

This philosophy allows us to get the four best linemen on the field. Obviously we will put linemen with the best feet at end. This system allows our third-best lineman to play inside or outside when a starter is injured.

ENDS

Defensive end play in high school football is very demanding. One week the end may have to defend the Wing-T and the next week, the veer option or the power I with its off-tackle power plays. The end will have to perfect a variety of techniques, such as tackling the dive, wrong arming off-tackle power plays, or playing off the guard's pin block in the Wing-T waggle. He must be a very versatile athlete. He must possess the bulk to defeat run blocks and the speed to rush the passer. The ends in our defense may be converted outside linebackers or safeties. In 1999 we had a converted third-team free safety make All-Conference at defensive end.

LINEBACKERS

Our linebackers are very active. They have multiple gap responsibilities depending on the front. They must be mobile enough to go out and play on air. Our linebackers must be able to cover backs. Our Bandit must be able to cover the tight end man to man. This allows us to free up the strong safety for other responsibilities. We stunt our linebackers quite a bit. We will stunt inside or outside. We are not blessed with a lot of speed, but our linebackers are mobile enough to do what we ask them to do. Our linebackers are the heart and soul of the defense. We have been fortunate to have one or more All-Conference selections each year for the past seven years. We have had several All-State picks, and in 1991 James Bates was named All-American. James went on to start at middle linebacker on the University of Florida National Championship team of 1996.

CORNERS

Basically our corners are involved in match coverage. Our corners will match up with the wideouts. Most of their practice time is spent on man coverage. We put our corners on an island a lot of times. This frees us to load up inside. Rarely do we ask our corners to have primary force. Occasionally we will crash stunt with our corners. We are able to do this with corners who are not overly fast. Most years our starters are in the 4.8 to 5.0 range in the 40-yard dash. We feel that what we are doing is effective. In 1999 we gave up an average of 38 yards passing per game during the regular season.

SAFETIES

In our base coverage, the safeties must be able to read the release of the number two receiver to their side. The safeties may supply help to the corner on number one or man cover number two according to the actions of number two. The safeties have primary force responsibility. On runs away, they have B gap to fold responsibility. The strong safety must be able to cover the tight end or a back man to man in our stunt package. In our Bears look, the strong safety must come out of the sky late and play in the box. In this position he will need some linebacker skills. The strong safety handles any break of formation in most of our coverages. In many of our stunt packages, the free safety has the first back out the weak side man to man. With an "Up"call, the safeties come down to linebacker depth. We do this when we want nine in the box. Again, blazing speed is not a requirement.

We feel that one of the secrets to defending the Wing-T is to have as much carryover as possible from the base defense. This is better than concocting a freak defense that has no relationship to what you normally do. I readily admit, however, that some refinements or changes are necessary when facing the Wing-T. As a rule we do not flip-flop our down linemen, but against the Wing-T, we will flip to some extent. Normally our linemen are in three-point stances, but versus the wing, we stand up our ends to help them vision their keys. We always flip our linebackers and secondary. We put our best cover corner on the split end and our best run corner to the wing. Normally our linebackers are aligned at 5 yards' depth, but versus the wing, we screw Sam down slightly to help him on traps. We also cheat Will more toward the call to help him on the buck trap. We also make an adjustment of slowing down the 3 technique because we were being influenced to death on the trap.

You should understand that the majority of our reads are the same regardless of the type of offense we face. The linebackers, for example, always key the fullback through the guard. This serves us well when we face the wing. Don't think we approach the wing passively. We talk constantly of keys and reads, but we are not a passive defense. When we read a particular key, we want to sell out and jump on the grenade. We always think attack, but first we have to know where to attack. We tell our players key and attack. If the key takes them to the wrong place, then it is our fault, not theirs. We stress "Trust your keys." Most teams seem to be mesmerized by all the ebb and flow of the Wing-T. What we try to stress is, when you read a particular key, sell out on the play. We will not accept timidity or being unsure. We do not tolerate players trying to find the ball because, obviously, with the ball-handling techniques incorporated in the Wing-T system, they will not find it. We feel this scheme is practical to any personnel situation. In a good year we might have a handful of players who run a sub 5.0 40-yard dash. We even teach this package to our freshmen. Superior personnel is not a requirement.

2

Understanding the Wing-T's Strengths and Weaknesses

The Wing-T was developed at the University of Delaware by Dave Nelson. The offense combines the principles of the Michigan single wing of Fritz Crisler and the Army trap series of Earl "Red" Blaik. After Nelson left the University of Iowa, he moved to the University of Delaware where he converted the Wing-T from being used primarily as a formation into an offensive system that is still evolving. Tubby Raymond has taken the mantle and today is the guru of the offense. To better attack the Wing-T, a defensive coach must be able to understand the strengths and weaknesses inherent in the system.

STRENGTHS

The Wing-T offense offers a great degree of multiplicity of formations, motions, shifts, and move to's. The one-step motion, red motion, flat red motion, and motion to and away from the formation present problems for the defense. The ebb and flow of the Wing-T can mesmerize the defense. Fast-flow defenses are susceptible to misdirection plays. Angle blocking with kickouts at the point of attack and a backside lead-through demoralizes the defense.

The Wing-T is proficient in attacking individual players who react to a certain play by attacking the player with a companion play that takes advantage of the technique he used to stop the previous play. The Wing-T advocates series football with multiple threats on each particular series. This philosophy can wear on a defense psychologically as well as physically. The Wing-T is basically a four-back offense because the QB can attack the perimeter to or away from flow. The fullback's alignment is ideal for quick-hitting plays on either side of the center. Perimeter problems are compounded with the positioning of the wing. Not only does this add an extra gap for the defense to defend, but it also makes the defense susceptible to being outflanked.

The passing game in the Wing-T is so dangerous because it is primarily play action in character. Defenders who overplay the run are subject to being burned on passes off the same run actions. The offense offers three quick receivers plus a fullback who is in position to release on either side of the ball. The positioning of the wing and tight end in close proximity can cause problems for man coverage with crossing routes. Play-action passes are effective not only because of defenders overplaying the run but also because the protection scheme is very solid. Another advantage that maybe is not as true as it used to be is that not many people run the Wing-T. In years past, defenses may have had to play one or two Wing-T teams yearly. The novelty of the offense caused problems. A major problem in preparing for the Wing-T is that not many scout teams can run the offense properly. Much defensive practice time is spent on coaching the service team.

WEAKNESSES

Like most offensive systems, the Wing-T has weaknesses, and like all multiple formation offenses, the Wing-T has formation tendencies. Despite all the window dressing, the offense can only snap the ball when it is in one of six possible formations, and only certain plays can be run with each formation. A well-coached defense can use this to its advantage if it understands that despite the multiplicity of formations, there are basically only four running series that most Wing-T teams run: 20 series—buck series; 30 series—power series; 40 series—no motion, or blue motion, belly series; and the wing motion series, which in this book is referred to as red motion. Diagram 2-1 illustrates the base Wing-T play with no motion, or blue motion. Diagram 2-2 illustrates the base Wing-T play with red motion.

If players are taught to focus on their particular key and reads, all the ebb and flow is not as confusing. Defenders must be taught where to look. Each defender must be like Odysseus and be restrained from the sweet sound and beauty of the Wing-T to avoid being smashed upon the rocks, which is the fate of most defenses that face the Wing-T.

A good scouting system will determine if the guards are equal in ability or if one is a better puller than the other or if one traps more effectively. How does the offense play to their particular strengths? This information is invaluable in game preparation. The same scrutiny

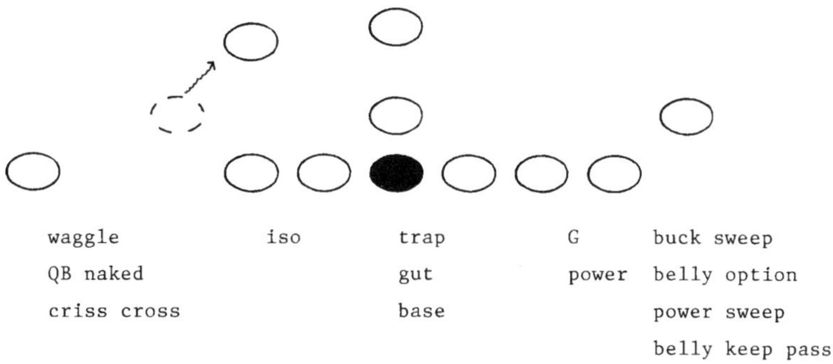

DIAGRAM 2-1
No Motion, or Blue Motion

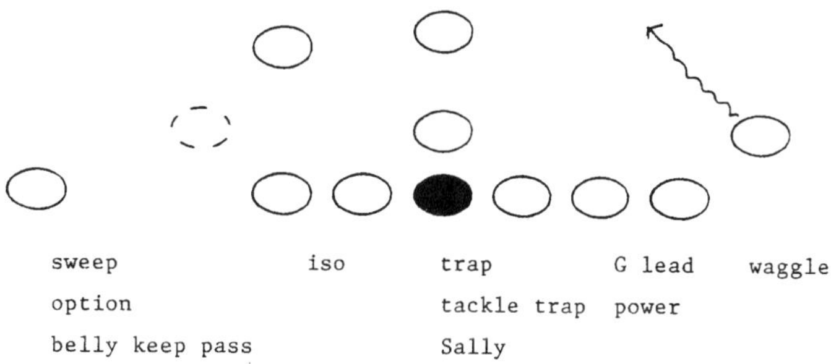

DIAGRAM 2-2
Red Motion

should be applied to the backs. A complete back in the Wing-T system must be able to block, run, and catch with equal skill. Seldom does this actually happen. How are their skills highlighted? Some teams will use a back strictly as a wing or a halfback. This gives the defense an advantage in preparation and recognition. Is the QB a better runner or thrower? The defensive coordinator can tailor his linebacker pass play to take away what the QB does best. The linebacker can be schemed to run through on waggles if the QB is more of a run threat and drop to help double receivers if the QB is a better thrower. It used to be that defenses might face one or two Wing-T teams a year. This made preparation difficult, but now, with the plethora of teams running the Wing-T, a defensive coach can use the same plan, with maybe a little tinkering, numerous times a year. This carryover effect is very beneficial because of the familiarity fostered by repetition.

3

Linebacker Play

This chapter deals with how Bandit, Sam, and Will play the Wing-T. It focuses on each position's keys and reactions to the various Wing-T series as it examines the no motion, blue motion, and red motion.

NO MOTION, OR BLUE MOTION, PLAYS

All linebackers key the fullback but underkey the guard to their side. Alignment vertically is 5 yards from the LOS, which allows us a good look at the key. Using the combination key of the fullback through the guard will tell us the play. If the linebackers get a conflict in their read, that is, if the guard goes one way and the fullback goes the other, they always go with the guard. See Diagram 3-1.*

Bandit's Reads vs. the 20 Series

If the guard blocks down and the fullback is away, the play is the down trap or a base give. Bandit will fit into the A gap. This is his normal backside fill read. See Diagram 3-2.

If the guard pulls to Bandit and the fullback is down the midline away, the Bandit must play sweep. The play might be the influence trap, but Bandit plays sweep. The nose, free safety, tackle, and Will play trap. See Diagram 3-3.

If the play is the buck sweep, Bandit will be the first defender to the POA. A mistake we made early on was to tell Bandit to fit over the top of the guard. When the guard would kick the Bandit and the corner came up outside, we would have two defenders outside the guard's block so in essence the guard was blocking two defenders. See Diagram 3-4.

**NOTE: Diagrams for Chapter 3 begin on page 14.*

The adjustment we made was to tell Bandit to either play the guard down the middle or play under the guard's block. See Diagram 3-5.

When both the fullback and the guard go away, Bandit plays screen or the tailback coming out the backdoor on a throwback. See Diagram 3-6.

Bandit's Reads vs. the 30 Series

On the power sweep, the fullback goes toward Bandit and the guard either doubles the tackle or folds. Treat either of the guard's blocks as a pull to. The Bandit should attack the fullback's block just as he does the guard's block on the buck sweep. He should play down the middle of the fullback or beat him underneath. See Diagram 3-7.

The companion play to the power sweep, the counter criss cross, is easily read by Bandit. The fullback will be to Bandit, but the guard will pull away. Remember, whenever there is a conflict, the guard overrides. Bandit in many cases will beat the back to the POA. See Diagram 3-8.

Bandit's Reads vs. the Belly Series

Bandit will get basically the same look on this series as he did on the 30 series power sweep. He wants to fit tight over the top of the wing. He should be over the top for the bounce out of the G scheme, or he would take the QB on the down option series. See Diagrams 3-9 and 3-10.

The end's reads will cause the G scheme to bounce because the end will far shoulder the guard. Bandit must beat the wing's block and take the QB on the down option. If Bandit mentally masters the combinations shown in Diagrams 3-11(a) through 3-11(f), he will contribute greatly to stopping the Wing-T offense.

Sam's Reads vs. the 20 Series

Sam will key the fullback and the same guard as Bandit. If the guard blocks down and the fullback is down the midline away, Sam follows his normal backside fill technique. Versus the down trap, all three linebackers will be a factor. In all, versus the down trap, we will have six defenders. See Diagram 3-12.

If the guard pulls to Sam and the fullback is down the midline away, Sam must play sweep. If the play is the influence trap, Will, the nose, the 3 technique, and the free safety have the responsibility to stop the play. With the influence scheme, Will is unblocked at the POA. If the offense wants to gut block the scheme, Will has to beat the guard there and attack him in the hole. See Diagram 3-13.

We tried to teach the Sam on this read to take a peek at the tackle on his way to sweep. If the play was a trap, the tackle would be upfield, and Sam needed to fall back inside for late help on the trap. If the offensive tackle blocked down on the defensive tackle, the play was the buck sweep. We were unable to get this done, but during the off season we plan to try it again. If both the fullback and guard pull away, Sam should man turn toward the tight end who is dragging on the waggle. He should use a catch technique and run with him. Sam is giving underneath help to the strong safety who has the tight end man. Versus a good running QB, the game plan may dictate that Sam be a run-through player on the QB versus the waggle. See Diagrams 3-14 and 3-15.

If the strong safety matches up well on the tight end and the QB is a definite run threat, it might be advisable to use Sam to counteract the running QB.

Sam's Reads vs. the 30 Series

Sam will see the same action Bandit sees on the power sweep series. If Sam gets both the guard and fullback to him, he plays inside out to the ball. However, if the fullback is to Sam but the guard pulls away, he will play the counter criss cross. We have played the criss cross two different ways with the Sam. The base way is to redirect to the POA. Most times he will have to contend with the playside offensive tackle. The tackle will work to Sam if Will has read his keys correctly and is over the top of the tackle's block. If Sam reads this play well, he can fit between the center's turnback block and guard's downblock on the nose. We have used both approaches. See Diagrams 3-16 and 3-17.

Sam's Reads vs. the Belly Series

As Sam reads his fullback and guard key, he can see peripherally the one- or two-step blue motion by the tailback. All the tailback is doing is motioning to the I formation. In most cases the play will be to the wing side. The Sally play is an exception. Sam, when he sees the flash of the tailback and the fullback's slide step, takes his eyes to the wing/tight-end area. The question Sam asks is, "What is the wing doing?" If the wing is downhill attacking the LOS, Sam will play inside out for the down option, G scheme, or belly keep pass. If the wing is counter stepping or drop steps, Sam will redirect and fall inside for the Sally. See Diagrams 3-18, 3-19, and 3-20.

Versus the Sally, Sam and the tackle will be unblocked at the POA. See Diagrams 3-21 and 3-22(a) through 3-22(f).

Will's Reads vs. the 20 Series

Will also reads the fullback, but he underkeys the weak guard. Normally Will plays in a 40 alignment, but to help him on the influence trap or gut trap, he needs to cheat to head up or a 30 on his guard. This adjustment may give him vision problems on seeing his guard, especially if the nose is a large player. If vision is a problem, the nose should be moved to a 1 technique.

If the fullback is down the midline to Will and the guard pulls away, he uses his normal free technique with a physical check. This is his basic read versus any offense. Will is a trap to sweep player with this read. See Diagram 3-23.

If the offense elects to gut block the play, Will must beat the guard to the POA. He must not allow the guard to square up in the hole. See Diagram 3-24.

Will can cheat on his alignment to get there quicker. If the offense elects to influence trap the 3 technique, Will is unblocked. See Diagram 3-25.

If the defensive tackle is in the hole, Will fits over the top for the spill out. The tackle's read gets him inside very quickly so he may get pinned by the guard. See Diagram 3-26.

Versus the down trap, the off guard will probably draw Will as his assignment. Since the 3 technique should be closing, there is little chance the ball will break back under the tackle to Will. With this in mind, Will should go over the top of the guard's block. If the ball does happen to break back weak, the free safety will clean up because he has B gap to fold on this backfield action. See Diagram 3-27.

If the play is the sweep, Will plays from trap to sweep.

With the fullback and guard to Will, he knows the play is the waggle. The fullback's path will probably be wider on his pass release. It is difficult to release down the midline because the nose is aligned in the A gap. Will assumes underneath coverage on the fullback with the free safety over the top. The free safety has primary coverage on the fullback with Will playing man under. Will can take chances on this route because the free safety is over the top. Jumping the flat route and shooting the hip are encouraged. See Diagram 3-28.

If the QB is a better run threat than passing threat, it might be better to use Will as a run-through player and expect the free safety to single cover the fullback.

Will's Reads vs. the 30 Series

On the power sweep, Will gets fast flow away by the fullback and his guard. There is little chance of a cutback, so Will has a mental check on the strongside A gap. See Diagram 3-29.

One of the best plays in the Wing-T system is the counter criss cross. This is a back breaker to a defense that fast flows.

Will has a great chance to make the play on the criss cross in this defensive scheme. The only time the guard will block down on the nose without red motion is on the criss cross. Even our third-team Will linebackers can read this. What Will sees is the fullback fast flow away but the guard block down. Will must understand that on the criss cross the tackle will block him. Will must get over the top of the tackle. The defensive end will wrong arm the play to Will. If everyone reads their keys, we have five defenders attacking the criss cross. See Diagram 3-30.

Will's Reads vs. the Belly Series

Will, as he keys the fullback and weak guard, will see the flash of the tailback's quick one- or two-step motion. His fullback key will slide step away. At this point Will checks the off area for the Sally. If the wing is downhill toward the LOS, he plays the run inside out. If the ball leaves the LOS, he gains width and depth on the belly keep pass. See Diagrams 3-31, 3-32, and 3-33(a) through 3-33(e).

RED MOTION READS

Bandit's Reads vs. Red Motion

We refer to wing motion as red motion. The wing must be to the strength call. When the corner gives a red call, Bandit takes his eyes to the strong guard. Bandit forgets about the fullback. If the guard pulls to Bandit, he is a run-through player for the red waggle. Stud will pull up the QB. Bandit will find a seam and take it to the QB. Bandit will try to beat the backside guard's block. If the QB is outside the Stud, Bandit will play over the top for second contain. See Diagram 3-34.

If the guard pulls away, Bandit plays trap to run away. See Diagram 3-35.

If the guard pass sets, Bandit has backside fill. If the defensive tackle plays it correctly, he will spill the play to Bandit. If the tackle is out on Bandit, he must hold leverage. See Diagram 3-36.

If the guard blocks down, Bandit will backside fill. See Diagram 3-37.

It is okay for Bandit to play over the top of the blocking scheme for the spill out of the trap by the 3 technique. If the QB takes the ball off the LOS, Bandit will gain depth looking for crossers. See Diagram 3-38.

Sam's Reads vs. Red Motion

Versus red motion, Sam keys the fullback. If the fullback is down the midline, Sam is coached to tackle him. The trap and the red waggle will have the same look to Sam. See Diagrams 3-39 and 3-40.

If it is the waggle, we have eliminated the fullback from the route. In essence the pattern is reduced to a three-man scheme instead of a four-man pattern.

Tackling the fullback allows the strong corner to give under help on the tight end instead of helping Sam with the fullback. If the fullback is wider than the midline on his release, Sam must jump him when he sifts through. Sam will have strong corner help on the fullback. See Diagram 3-41.

On the red trap, Sam will be unblocked if he beats the tackle's block. See Diagram 3-42.

One of the possible blocking adjustments would be to shoeshine the 3 technique and put the center on Sam. If this happens, the 3 technique should be screwed down to a 0 on the guard. If the play is the sweep, Sam will play trap to sweep.

If the fullback goes away from Sam, Sam takes his eyes to the tailback. This is a carryover on our basic split-back read when our key goes away, so there is no new teaching. The tailback will now tell Sam the play. If the tailback rock steps or does not attack the LOS, Sam plays counter. See Diagram 3-43.

If the tailback attacks the LOS, Sam will play inside out for the iso, option, sweep, and so forth. If the QB takes the ball to the second level, Sam will get deep looking for crossers.

Will's Reads vs. Red Motion

With red motion, Will keys the tailback. If the tailback attacks the LOS, Will matches the tailback's angle for the iso, sweep, option, or pass. If the tailback counter steps or does not attack the LOS, Will beats him to the POA. Will takes the QB on the option. See Diagrams 3-44, 3-45, and 3-46.

On the belly keep pass, Will can take a chance because the free safety is over the top of the tailback. See Diagram 3-47.

Diagrams 3-48 and 3-49 show Will's reactions to counter plays.

On the red waggle, Will walls the tailback's inside shoulder, man turns on him, and plays him hard underneath. The free safety has him over the top. See Diagram 3-50.

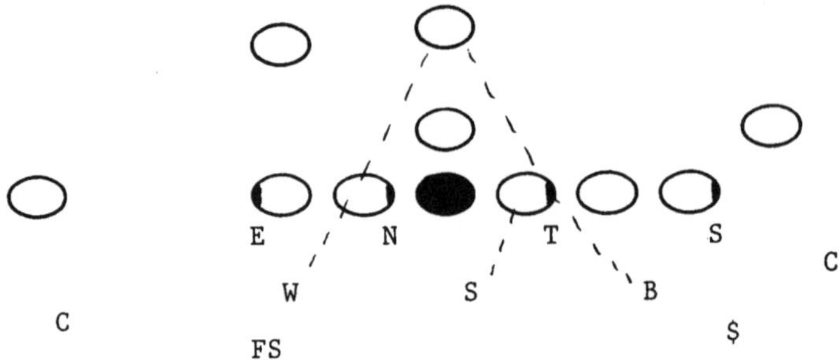

DIAGRAM 3-1
Linebacker Keys

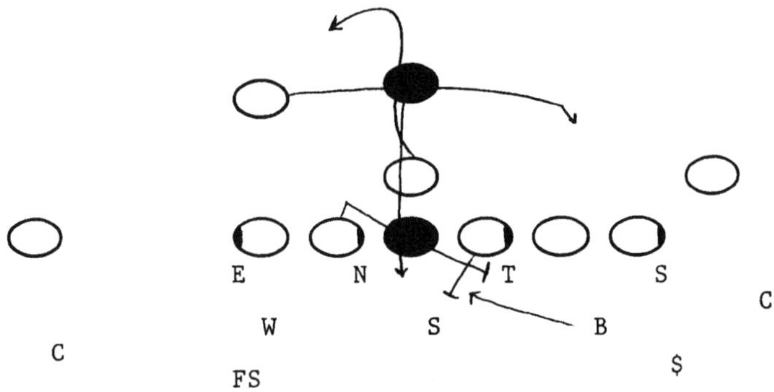

DIAGRAM 3-2
Down Trap

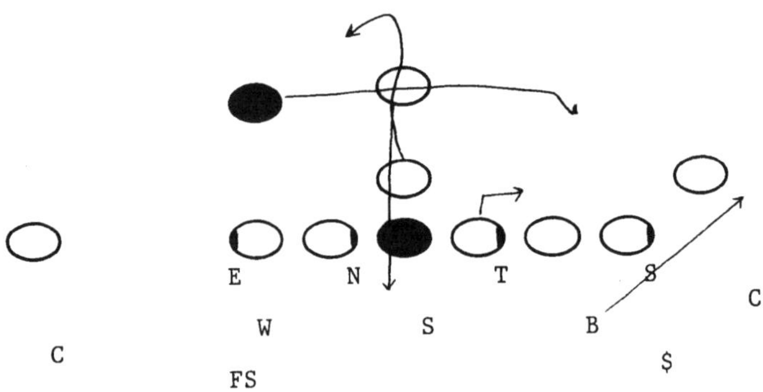

DIAGRAM 3-3
Sweep Read

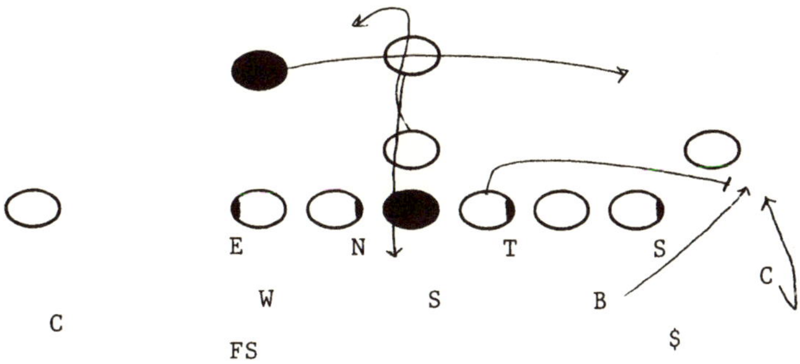

DIAGRAM 3-4
Incorrect Bandit Force

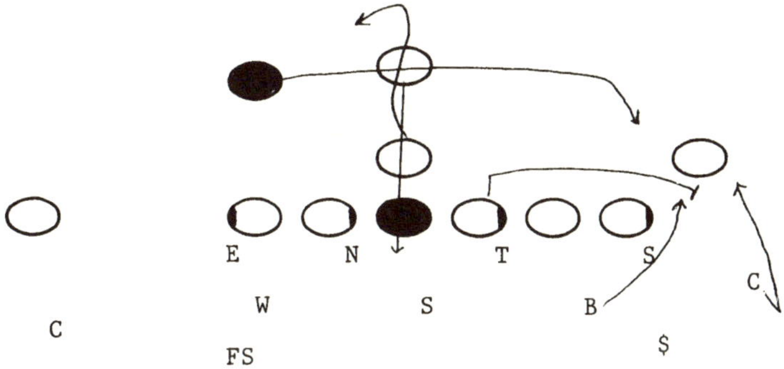

DIAGRAM 3-5
Correct Bandit Force

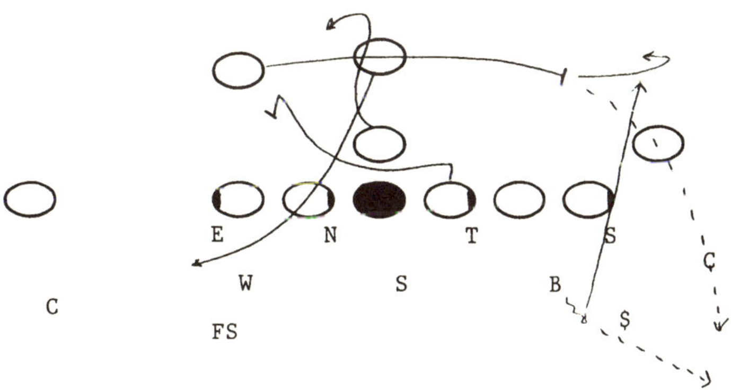

DIAGRAM 3-6
Bandit's Waggle Responsibility

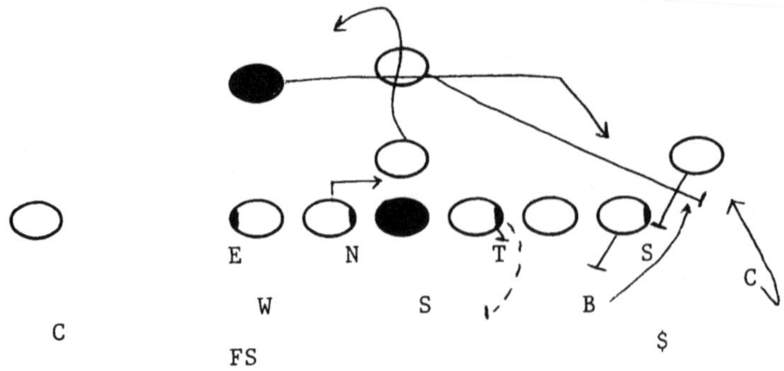

DIAGRAM 3-7
Power Sweep

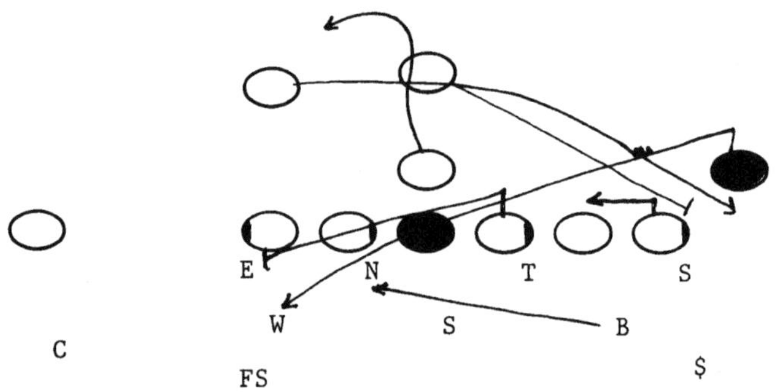

DIAGRAM 3-8
Counter Criss Cross

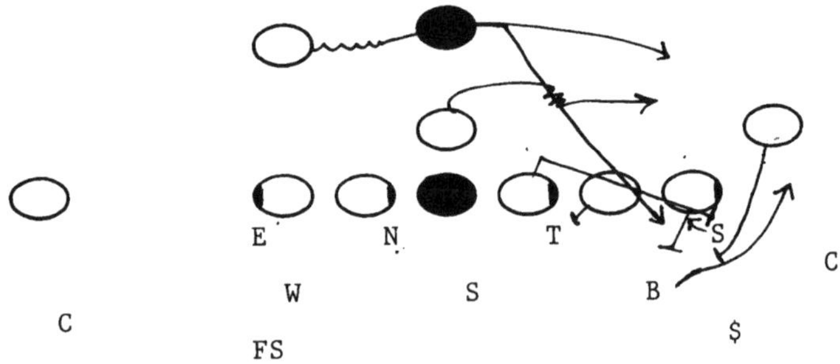

DIAGRAM 3-9
G Scheme

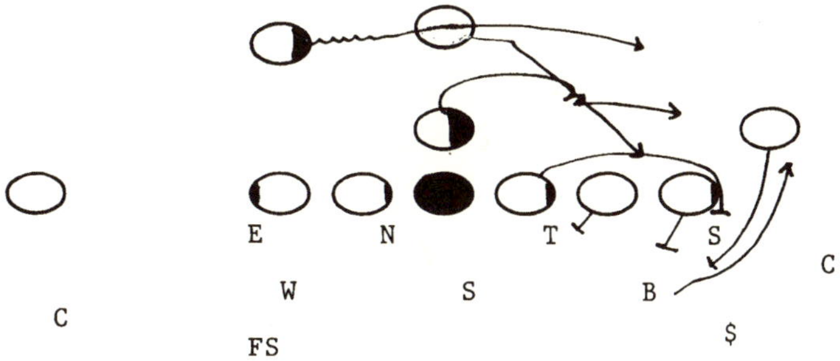

DIAGRAM 3-10
Belly Option

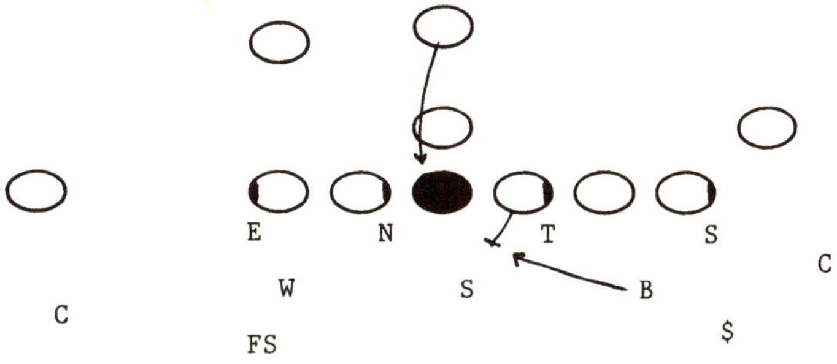

DIAGRAM 3-11(a)
Bandit's Reads—Down Trap

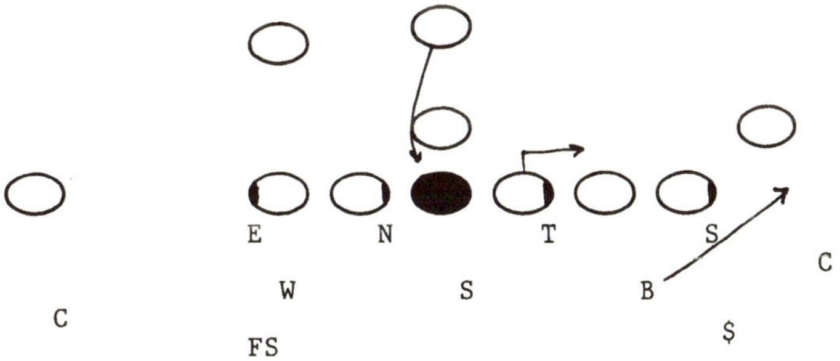

DIAGRAM 3-11(b)
Bandit's Reads— Sweep

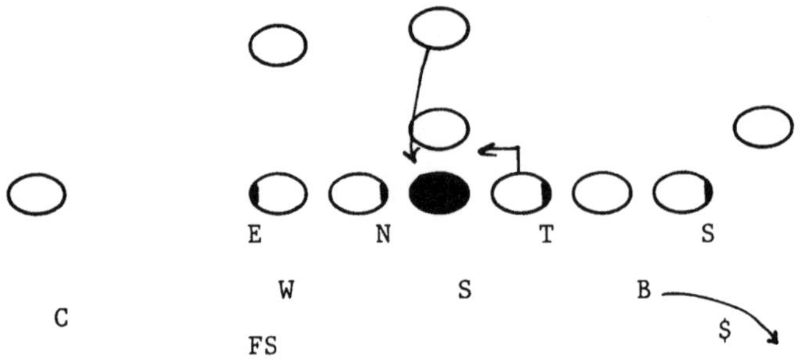

DIAGRAM 3-11(c)
Bandit's Reads — Waggle

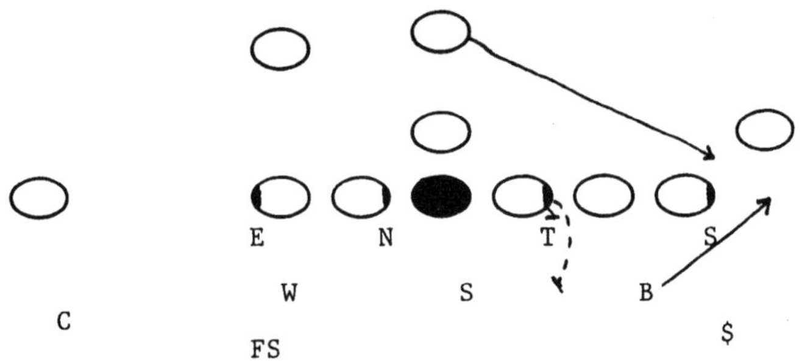

DIAGRAM 3-11(d)
Bandit's Reads — Power Sweep

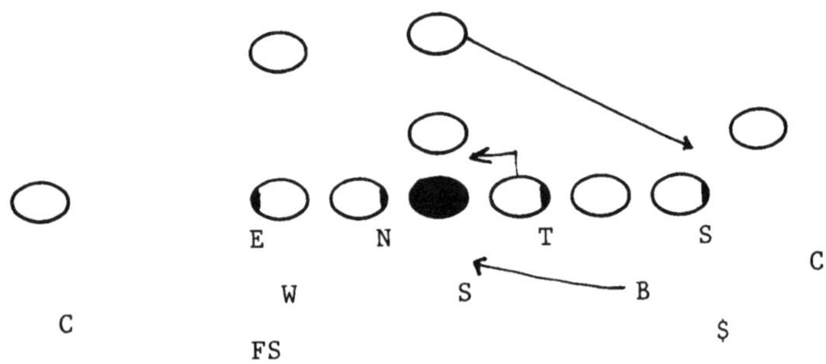

DIAGRAM 3-11(e)
Bandit's Reads — Criss Cross

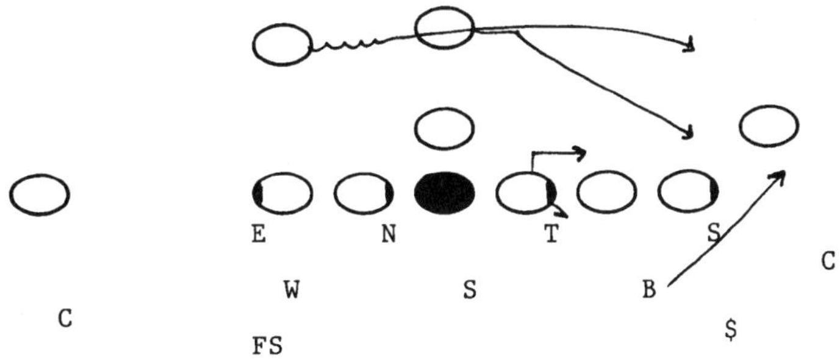

DIAGRAM 3-11(f)
Bandit's Reads — Belly

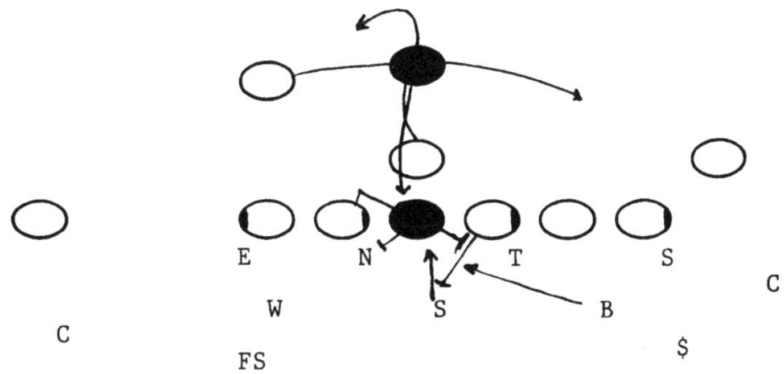

DIAGRAM 3-12
Down Trap

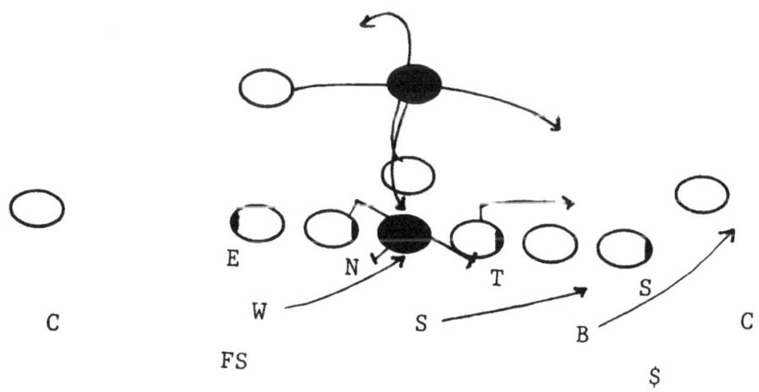

DIAGRAM 3-13
Influence Trap

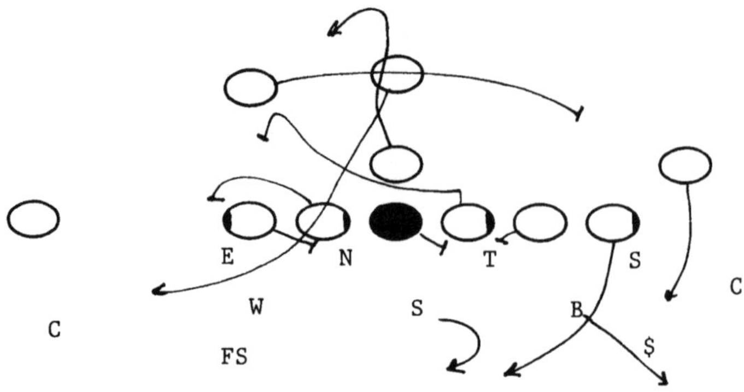

DIAGRAM 3-14
Waggle Drop

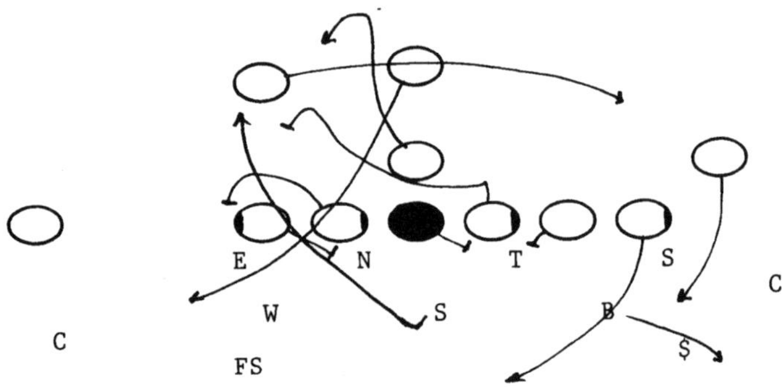

DIAGRAM 3-15
Waggle Run-through

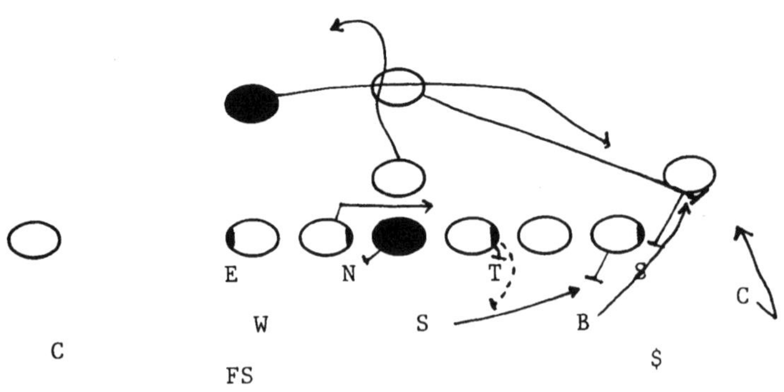

DIAGRAM 3-16
Power Sweep

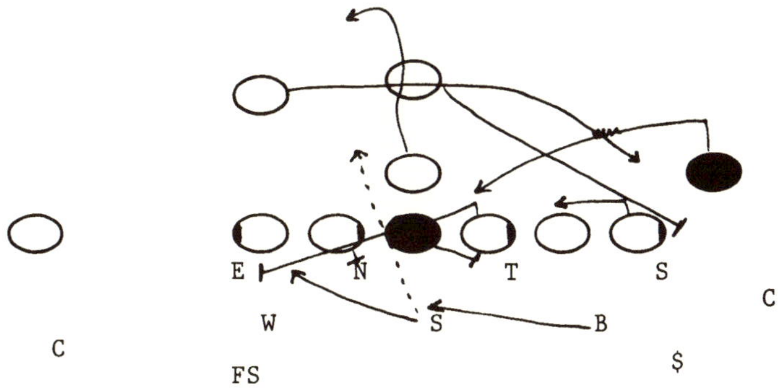

DIAGRAM 3-17
Criss Cross

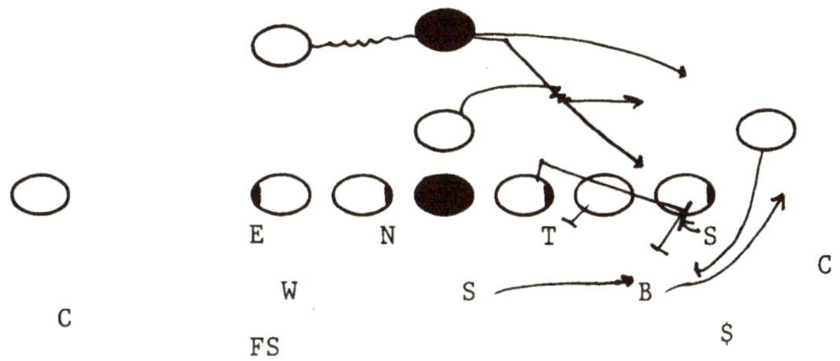

DIAGRAM 3-18
G Scheme

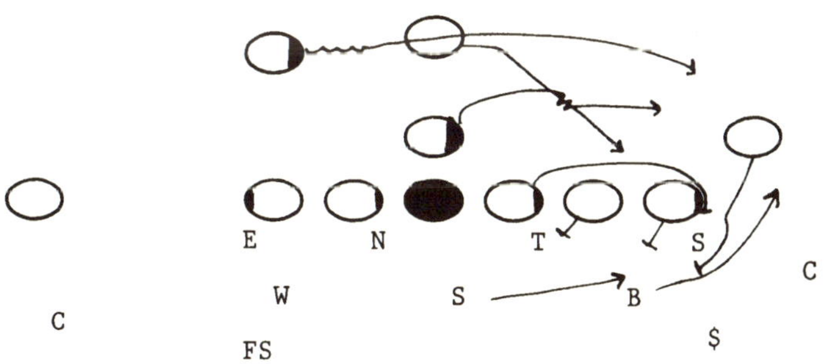

DIAGRAM 3-19
Belly Option

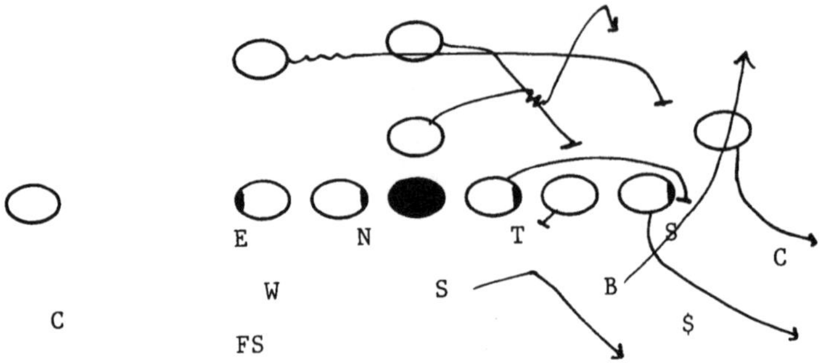

DIAGRAM 3-20
Belly Keep Pass

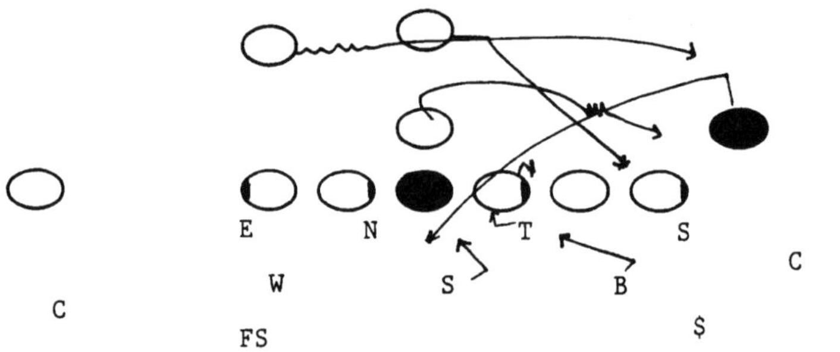

DIAGRAM 3-21
Sally

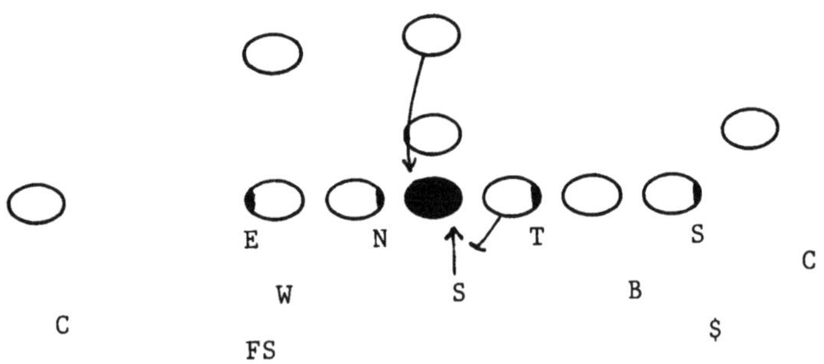

DIAGRAM 3-22(a)
Sam's Reads — Down Trap

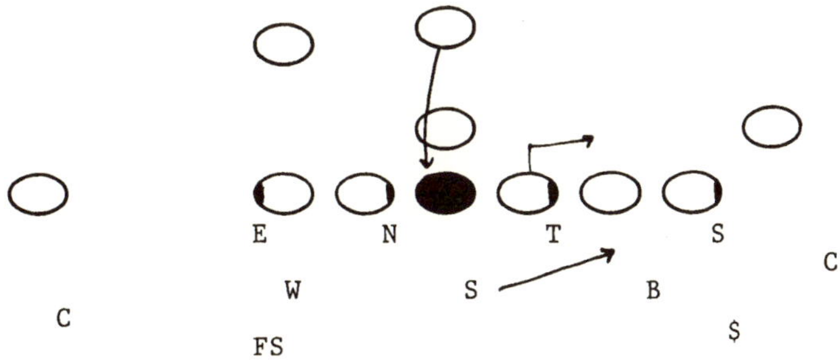

DIAGRAM 3-22(b)
Sam's Reads — Sweep

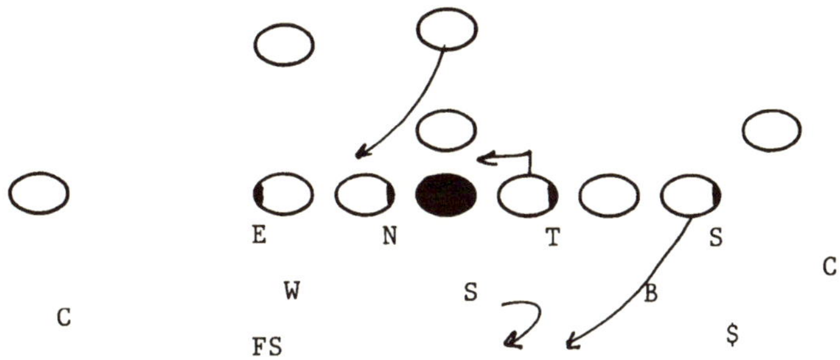

DIAGRAM 3-22(c)
Sam's Reads — Waggle

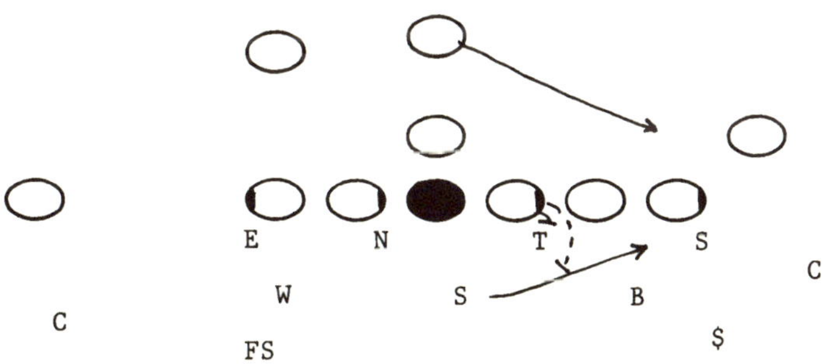

DIAGRAM 3-22(d)
Sam's Reads — Power Sweep

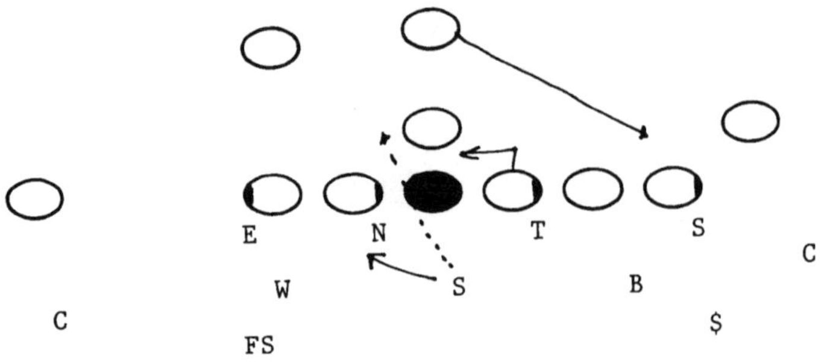

DIAGRAM 3-22(e)
Sam's Reads — Criss Cross

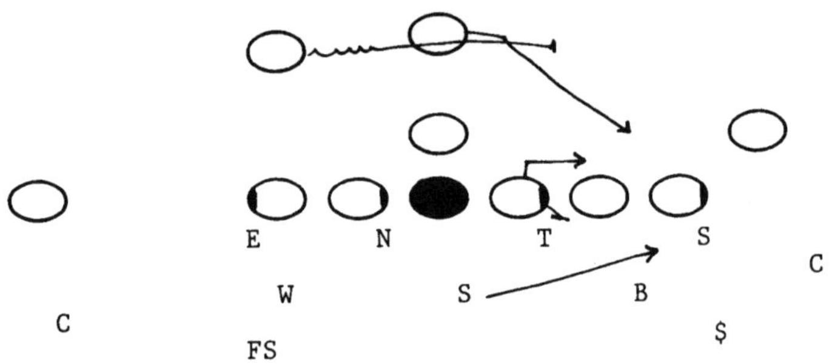

DIAGRAM 3-22(f)
Sam's Reads—Belly

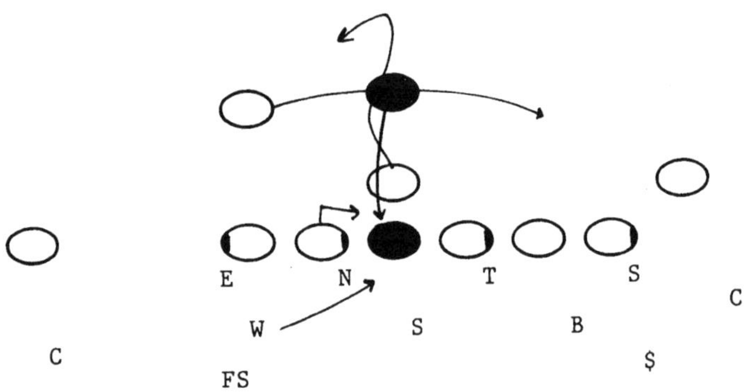

DIAGRAM 3-23
Trap Read

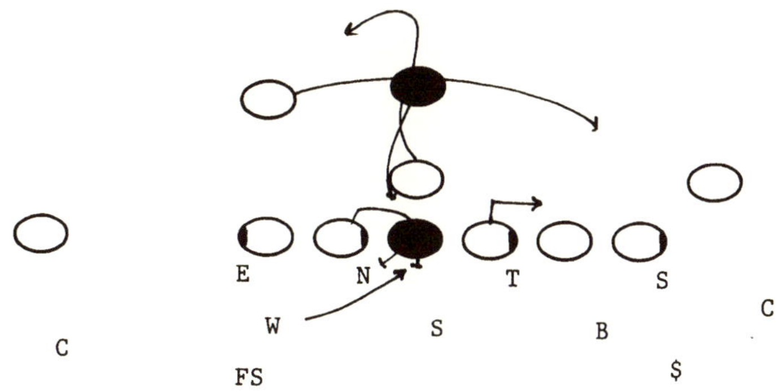

DIAGRAM 3-24
Gut Block

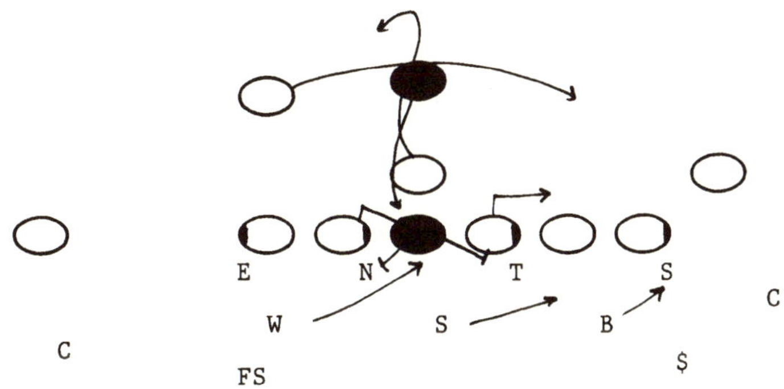

DIAGRAM 3-25
Influence Trap — Will Unblocked

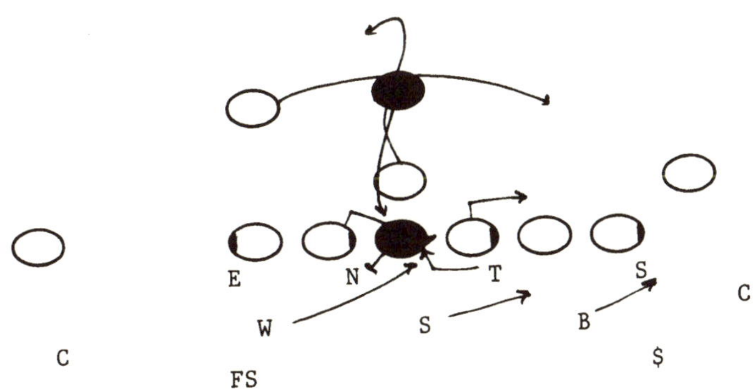

DIAGRAM 3-26
Influence Trap — Will Over the Top for Spill Out

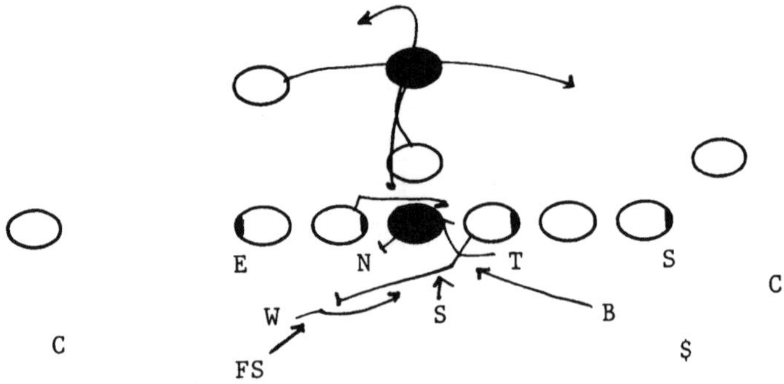

DIAGRAM 3-27
Down Trap

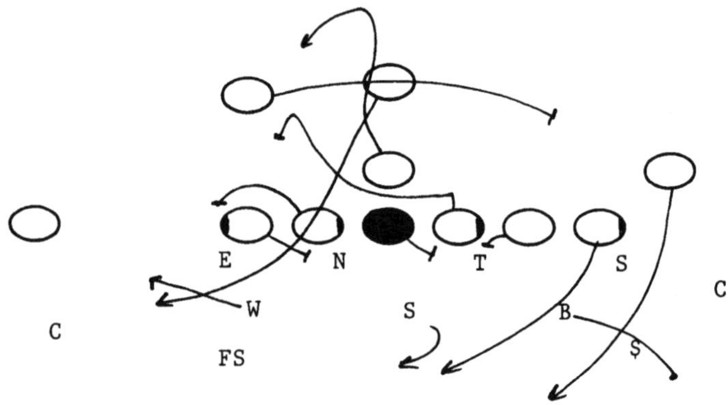

DIAGRAM 3-28
Waggle

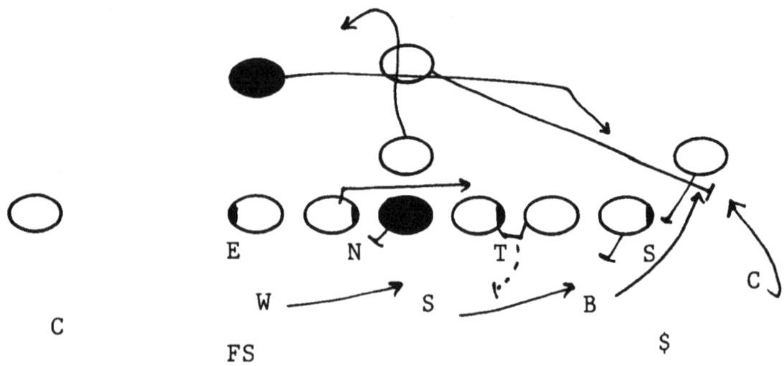

DIAGRAM 3-29
Power Sweep

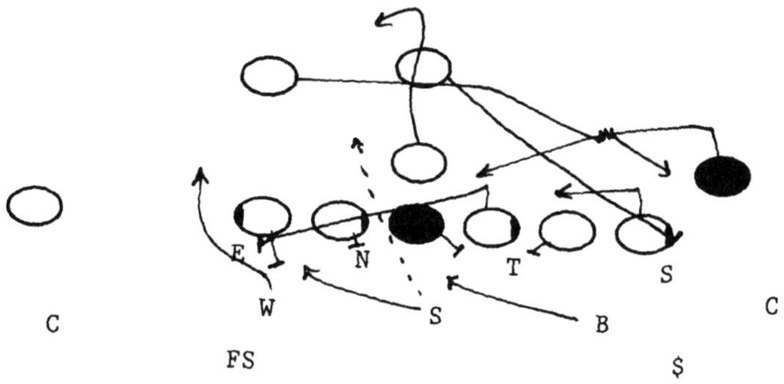

DIAGRAM 3-30
Counter Criss Cross

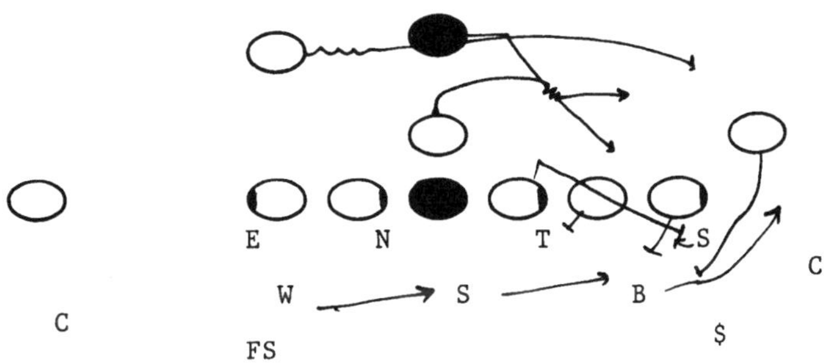

DIAGRAM 3-31
Belly

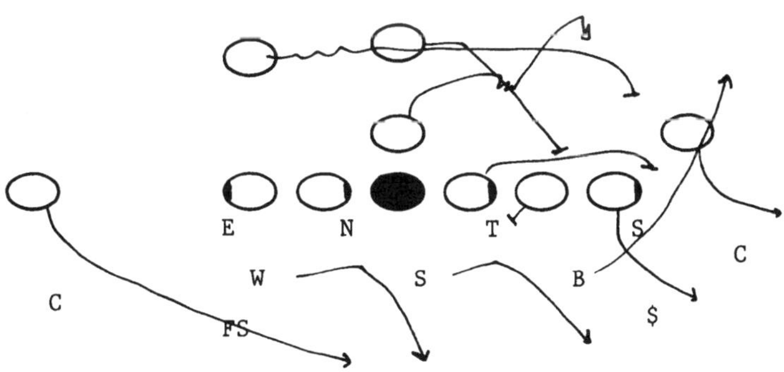

DIAGRAM 3-32
Belly Keep Pass

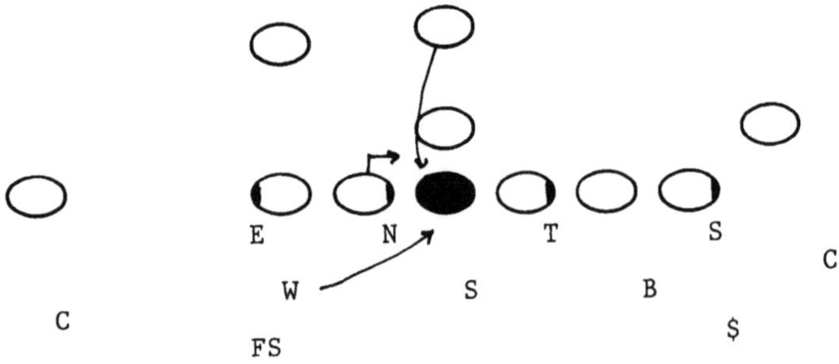

DIAGRAM 3-33(a)
Will's Reads — Trap

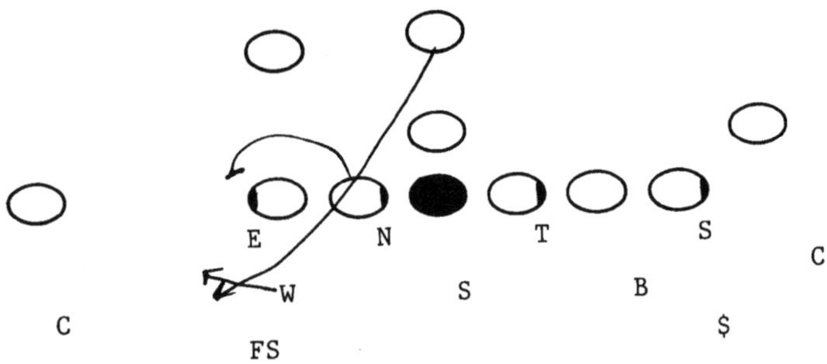

DIAGRAM 3-33(b)
Will's Reads — Waggle

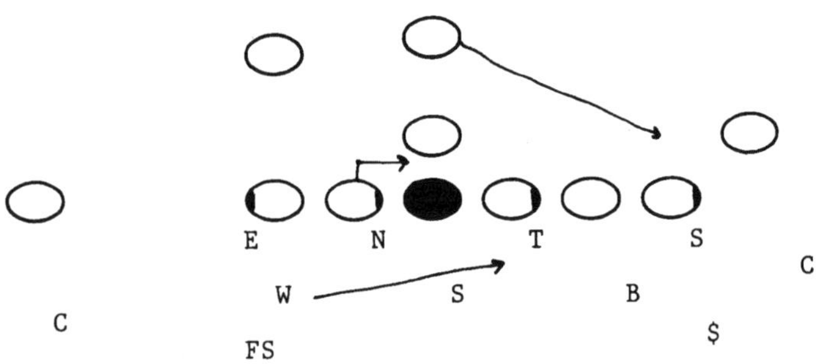

DIAGRAM 3-33(c)
Will's Reads — Power Sweep

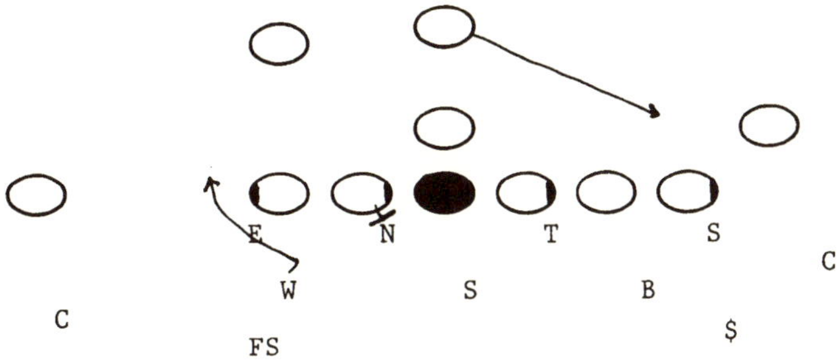

DIAGRAM 3-33(d)
Will's Reads — Criss Cross

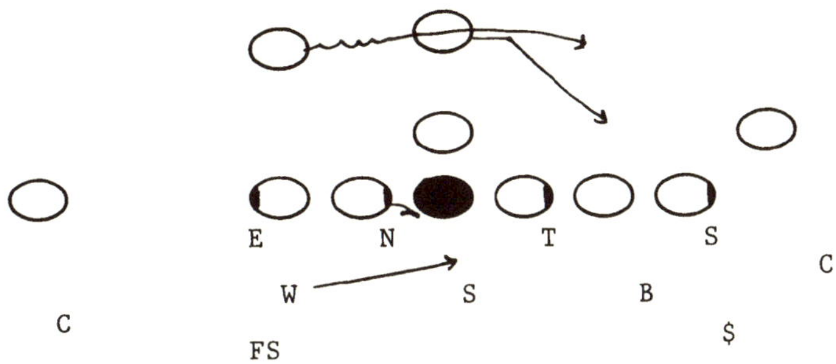

DIAGRAM 3-33(e)
Will's Reads — Belly

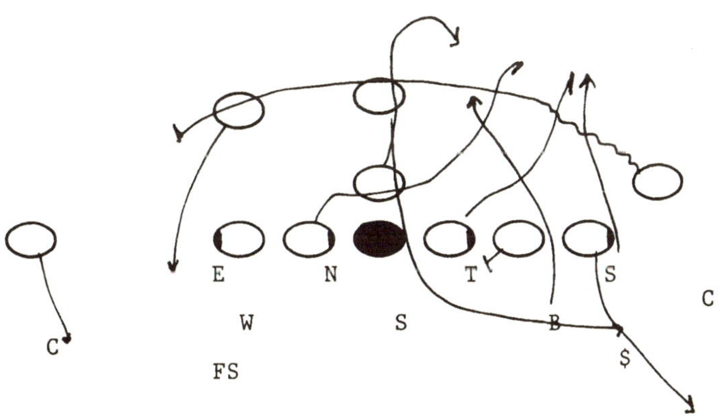

DIAGRAM 3-34
Red Waggle

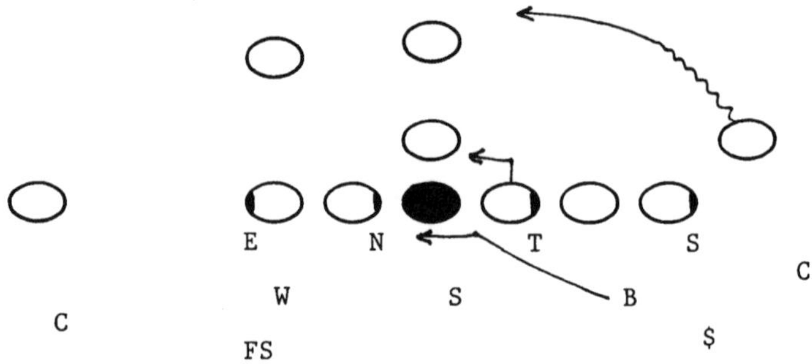

DIAGRAM 3-35
Trap/Sweep

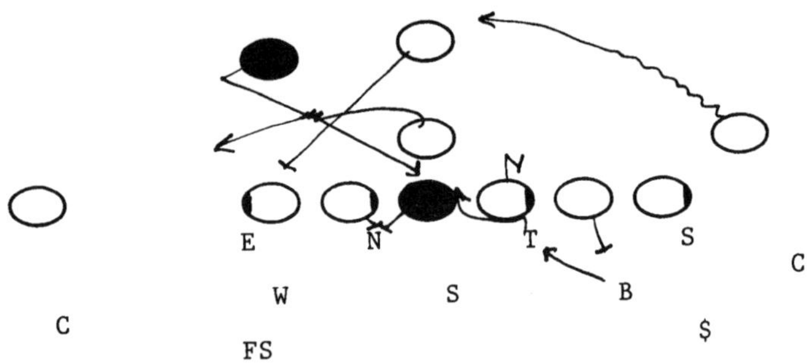

DIAGRAM 3-36
Sally

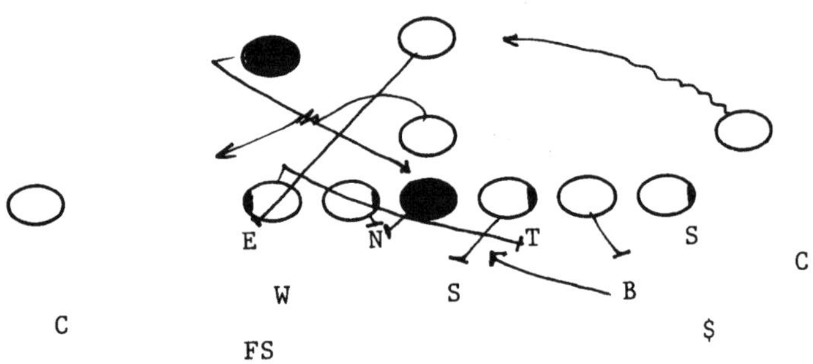

DIAGRAM 3-37
Tackle Trap

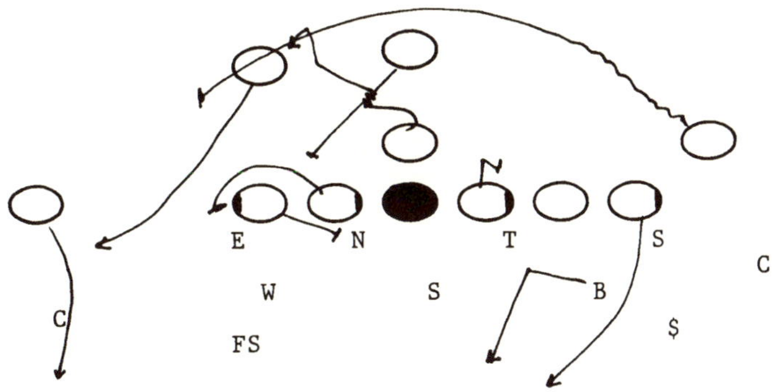

DIAGRAM 3-38
Belly Keep Pass

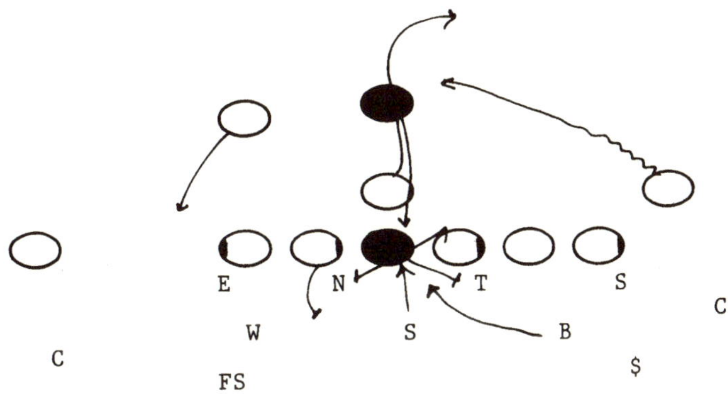

DIAGRAM 3-39
Red Trap

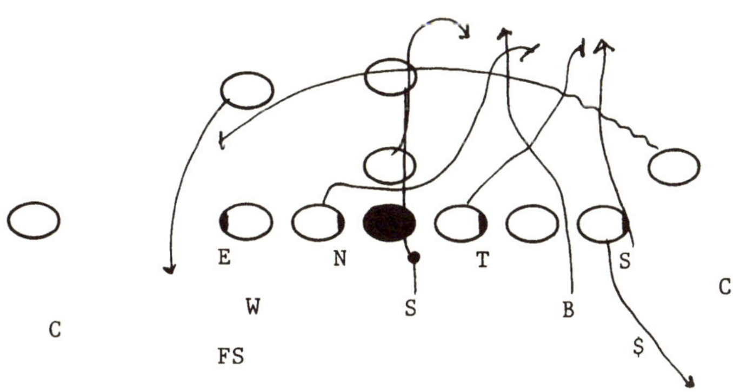

DIAGRAM 3-40
Red Waggle—Fullback Down the Midline

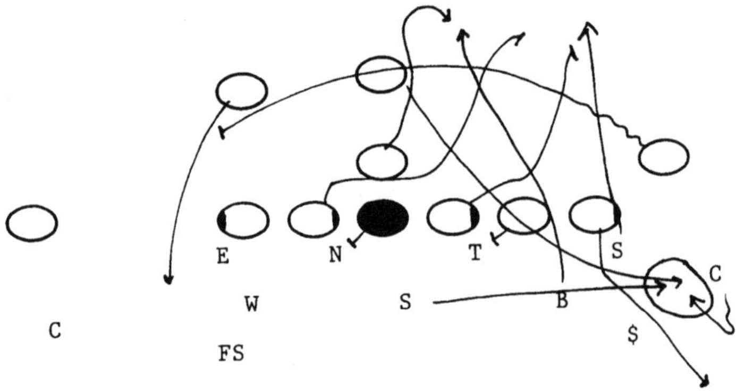

DIAGRAM 3-41
Red Waggle—Fullback Wide

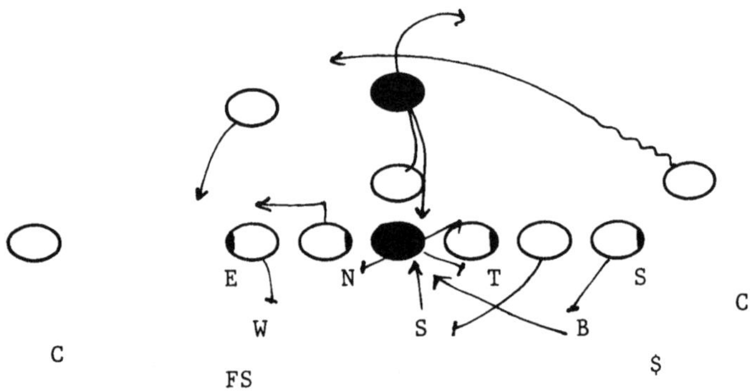

DIAGRAM 3-42
Red Trap

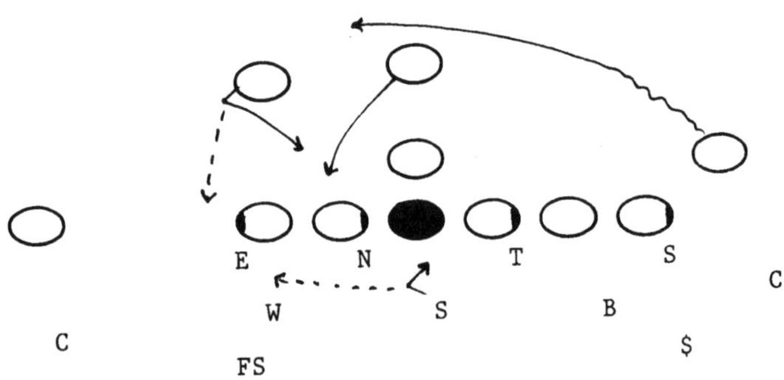

DIAGRAM 3-43
Fullback Goes Away From Sam

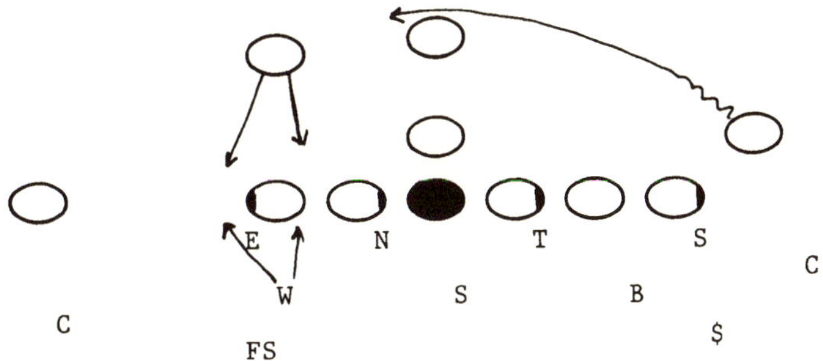

DIAGRAM 3-44
Will Matches Tailback's Angle

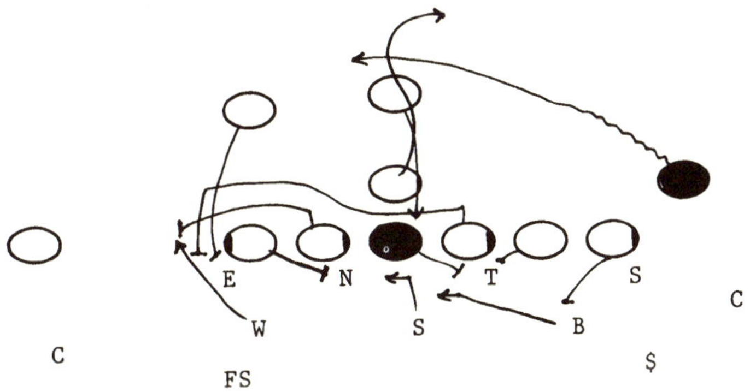

DIAGRAM 3-45
Sweep

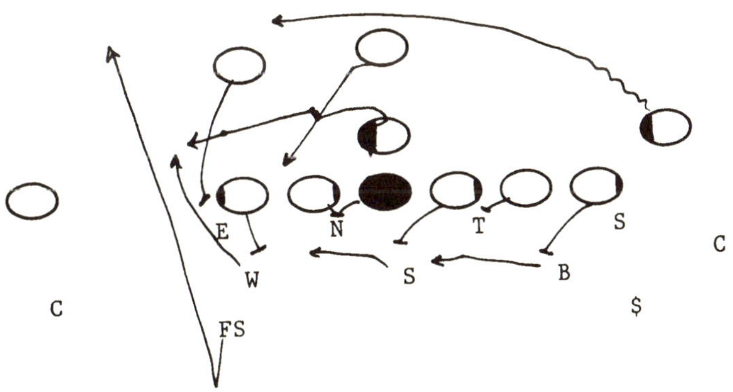

DIAGRAM 3-46
Red Option

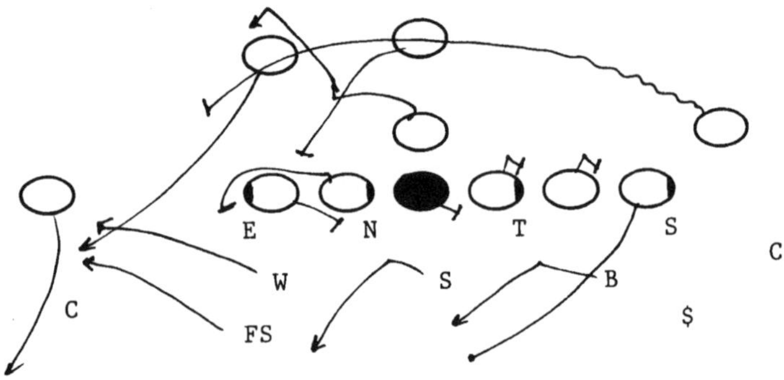

DIAGRAM 3-47
Belly Keep Pass

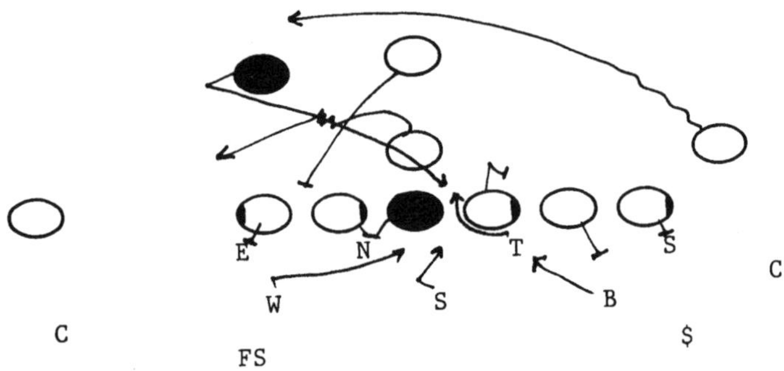

DIAGRAM 3-48
Sally

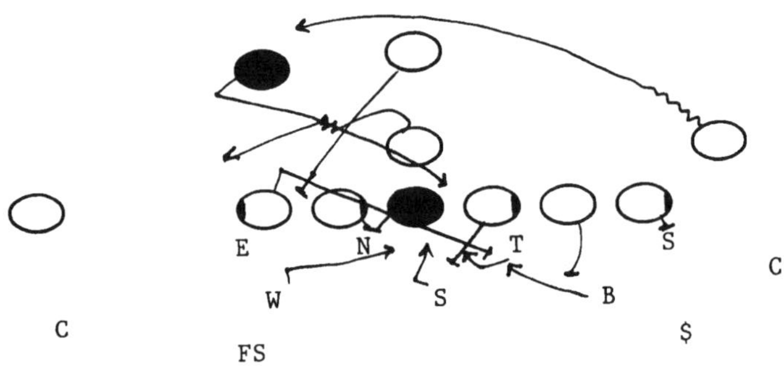

DIAGRAM 3-49
Tackle Trap

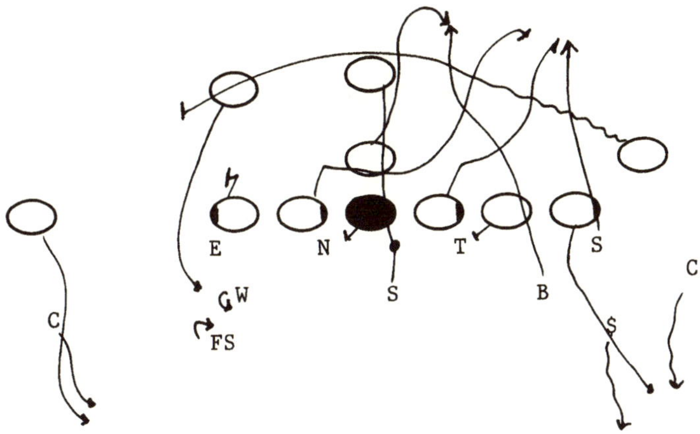

DIAGRAM 3-50
Red Waggle

4

Tackle Play

Responsibility-wise, tackle play in this package is the easiest. Ideally it is better to have the quicker of the two tackles play away from the call and use a larger, more physical player to the call. The ideal situation would be to have a reader to the call and a penetrator away from the call. Normally we are an attack-first, read-second defensive front, but the Wing-T can false key and influence the 3-technique tackle. We have learned the hard way that we had to make a change versus Wing-T teams. The 2 technique's assignment is very simple—his only job is to penetrate. There are no reads to master. His one and only technique is to see the ball—and when it wiggles, come off a hundred miles an hour. His job is to penetrate and hopefully knock off a puller. We understand he will be trapped on the red trap, but that is Sam's play to make.

THE 3 TECHNIQUE'S READS

We tell the 3 technique that his job is to play the trap. Play trap first, then find the ball. We tighten him down on the guard horizontally, but vertically we get separation from the LOS. We get into a more balanced stance with a 50/50 weight distribution. His visual key is the guard, but he sees the offensive tackle peripherally.

The 3 technique will close and wrong arm the trap. One problem with the down trap is that we sometimes close too flat to the LOS. This makes it easy for the guard to pin us. We want to close and at the same time get upfield so the fullback will have to run the hump on his bounce out. See Diagrams 4-1, 4-2, and 4-3.

Versus the down trap, we should have all three linebackers, the 3-technique tackle, the nose, and the free safety on the play. This gives us six defenders should the offense decide to trap us in this manner.

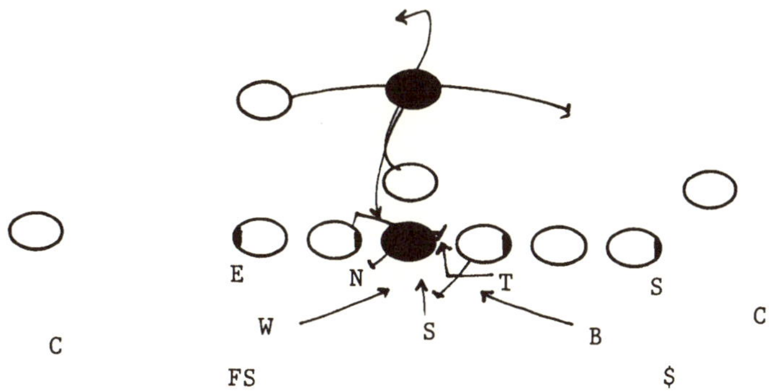

DIAGRAM 4-1
Down Trap

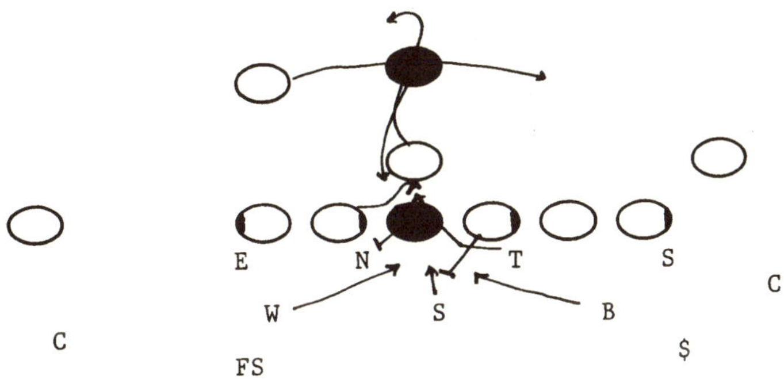

DIAGRAM 4-2
Correct Way to Wrong Arm the Trap

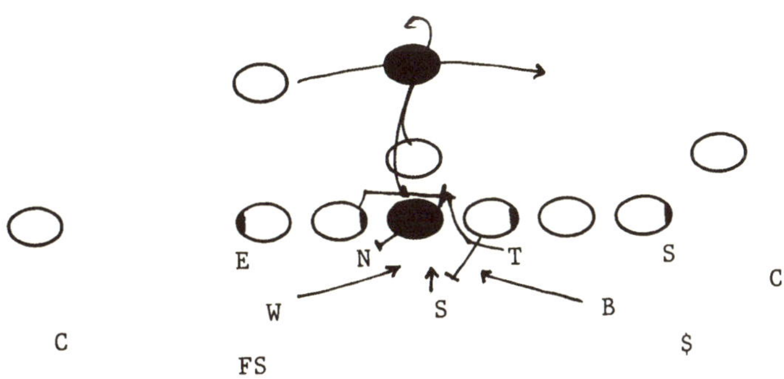

DIAGRAM 4-3
Incorrect Way to Play the Trap

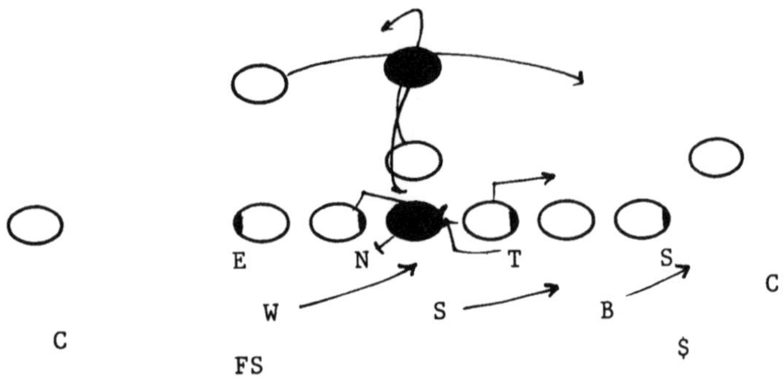

DIAGRAM 4-4
Influence Trap

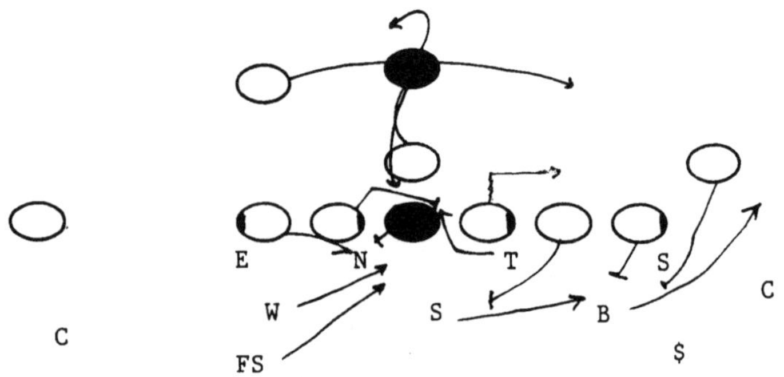

DIAGRAM 4-5
Influence Trap Pass Set

We treat an outside pull by the guard as a trap until we feel a down block by the offensive tackle. It is understood that the tackle will be blocked on the sweep, but how many times will he make the play on the 20 series sweep anyway? See Diagrams 4-4 and 4-5.

Versus this trap scheme, Bandit and Sam will play sweep. This leaves us with four trap players—Will, the free safety, the nose, and the 3 technique. Since we lost Sam and Bandit, we cannot allow the fullback to work too quickly away from Will by giving the fullback a shallow bounce-out route over the top of the 3 technique. It is imperative that we get depth by the 3 technique on his far-shoulder technique. See Diagram 4-6.

We often see a true pass set by the guard. The guard invites the tackle to make an upfield rush. Treat this as an influence trap and come under this block. See Diagram 4-7.

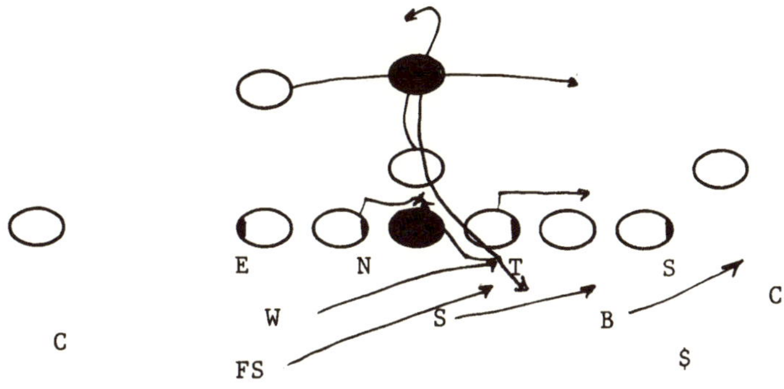

DIAGRAM 4-6
Desired Fullback Bounce-Out Route

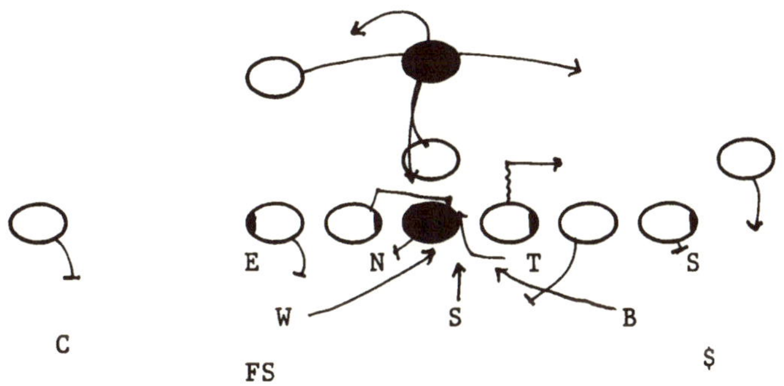

DIAGRAM 4-7
Pass Set Influence Trap

This influence-trap technique has been effective against teams that try to Sally scheme the defense. As you can see, we will be unblocked at the POA if we come under the guard's block. See Diagram 4-8.

If the guard pulls away, a turnback block by the center should be expected. The tackle should tight cross-face this turnback block. If there is no red motion, chances are the play is the waggle. See Diagram 4-9.

The tackle cross-faces the turnback block and gets north. When the end pulls the QB up, the 3 technique has a chance for a sack on the QB. We have had several sacks because the 3 technique fits in between the nose and the defensive end. The offensive tackle blocks the nose, and if the end does his job, both guards will try to block him. The guards have their back to the backside 3 technique. With the QB in the cylinder, the tackle has a chance for a big play.

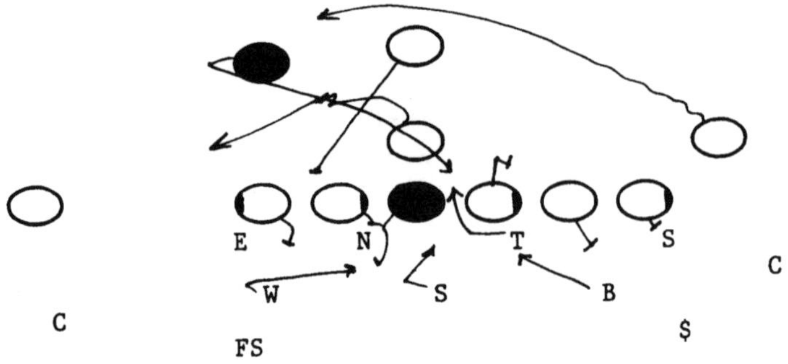

DIAGRAM 4-8
Sally

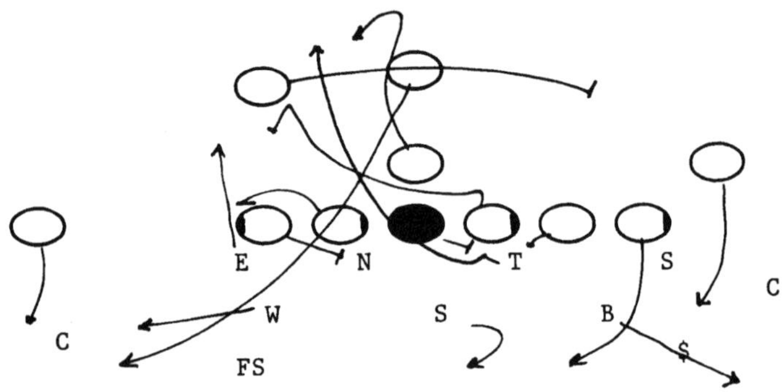

DIAGRAM 4-9
Guard Pulls Away on Waggle

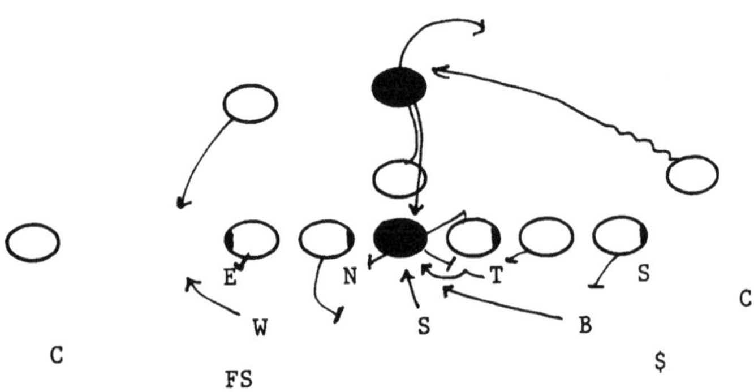

DIAGRAM 4-10
Red Trap

On the red motion trap, the center will turn back on the 3 technique. The tackle will be a factor on this play if he cross-faces. See Diagram 4-10.

THE 2 TECHNIQUE'S PLAY

As was stated earlier, the nose's assignment is to get penetration. The nose is coached to crowd the ball and take the A gap on the snap. He does this with the understanding that on both the 20 series sweep and the trap, he will get a turnback block by the center and in all probability will run around these blocks and will have to chase the ball backdoor. But again, how many plays will he make anyway since the center has the advantage of angle? Unless the nose is superior physically to the center, not many plays will be made. The third phase of the 20 series is dramatically affected by penetration from the nose. The offensive tackle has an uphill block on the waggle. If the nose is quick enough, he will give the offensive tackle fits trying to down block him. See Diagram 4-11.

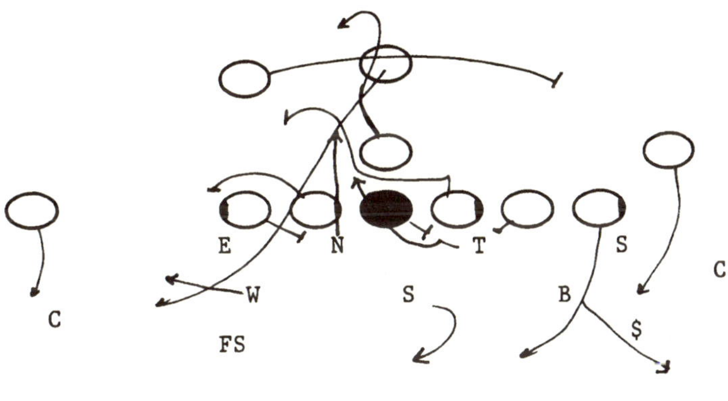

DIAGRAM 4-11
Waggle

If the nose is moved to a 1 shade on the center, this makes the tackle's job even harder. Most teams will have to change their waggle-blocking scheme to a "solid" look to get the nose blocked. The trade-off, however, is that the offense has no chance of getting a pin on the defensive end. This eliminates the threat of a run by the QB. See Diagram 4-12.

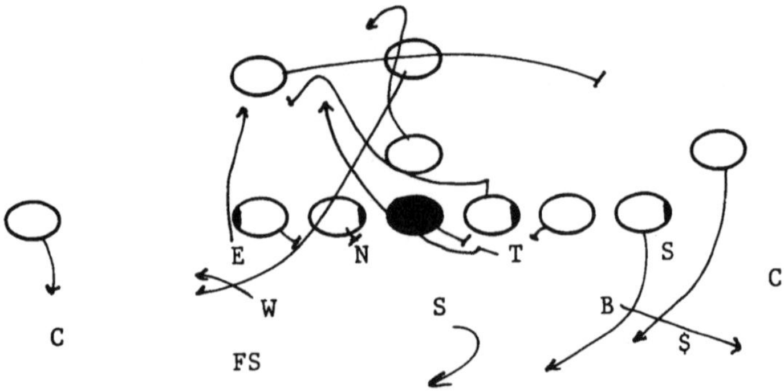

DIAGRAM 4-12
Solid Waggle Scheme

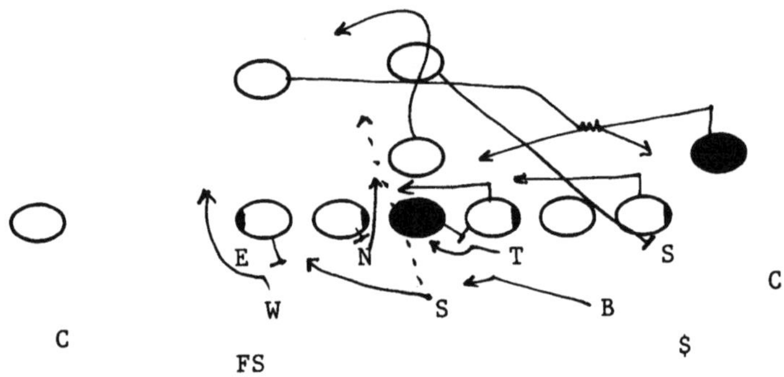

DIAGRAM 4-13
Counter Criss Cross

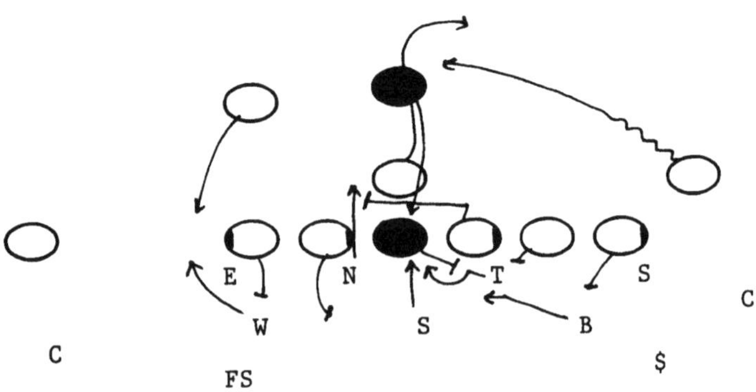

DIAGRAM 4-14
Red Trap

Penetration by the nose will destroy the criss cross off the power sweep series. See Diagram 4-13. Penetration is really effective versus the red motion series.

The nose will be blocked on the red trap; however, Sam will make the play because he is unblocked. See Diagram 4-14.

The nose presents the tackle with the same problem on the red sweep as he did on the waggle. It is difficult to block down on him and prevent penetration. At the least we expect the nose to knock off the backside guard. An adjustment the offense may make is to pull the tackle and block down on the nose with the guard. This, however, raises the question of who is the better puller—the guard or the tackle? See Diagram 4-15.

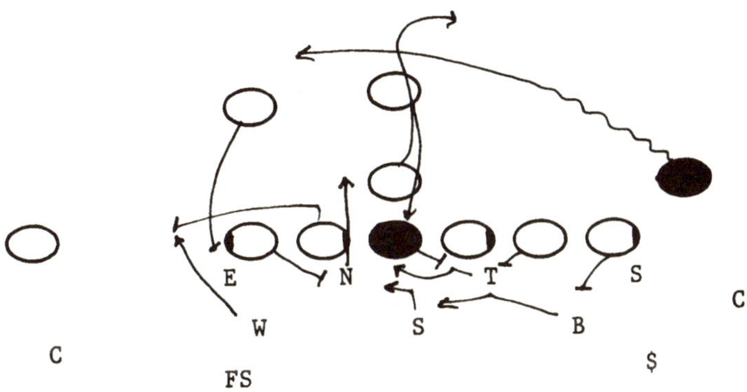

DIAGRAM 4-15
Red Sweep

5

End Play

Ideally we want the larger, more physical end to the call and the smaller, quicker end away from the call. If both ends are similar in style of play, the end with the best feet goes to the weak side.

Normally we have our ends in a three-point, cocked stance with their inside hand down and inside foot back. Versus the Wing-T, we use a two-point stance with the inside foot back, and on the snap we take a power step with that foot. To the call we use what we term a "chew" technique. This is a tight 9 technique: the end feels the tight end and looks at the fullback. See Diagram 5-1.

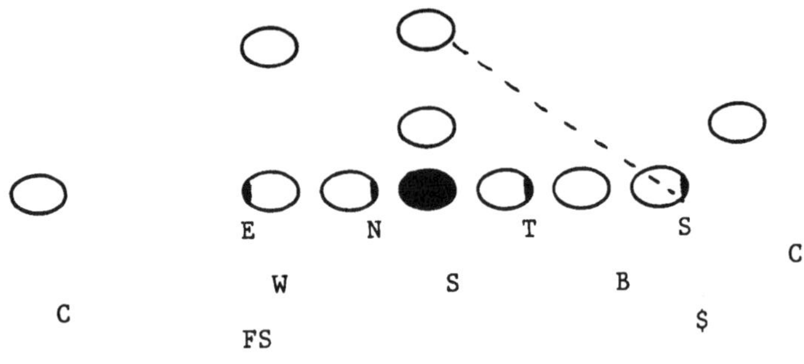

DIAGRAM 5-1
Stud's Key

STUD'S READS

If the tight end bases, the end thinks double team and tries to get a push upfield. See Diagram 5-2.

With an outside release by the tight end, the end thinks pass; the fullback will probably block him. See Diagram 5-3.

As the end feels the tight end block down and sees the fullback go away, he should think sweep and expect the wing to block down. He should attack and two gap the wing. He tries to knock him back and force the ball to bounce or at least make the backside guard run the hump. See Diagram 5-4.

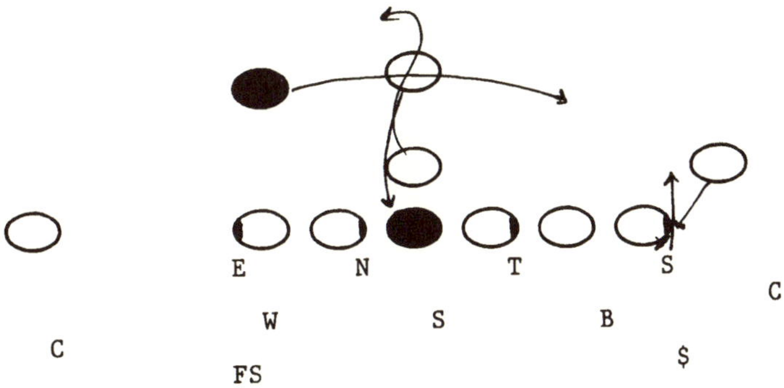

DIAGRAM 5-2
Double Team

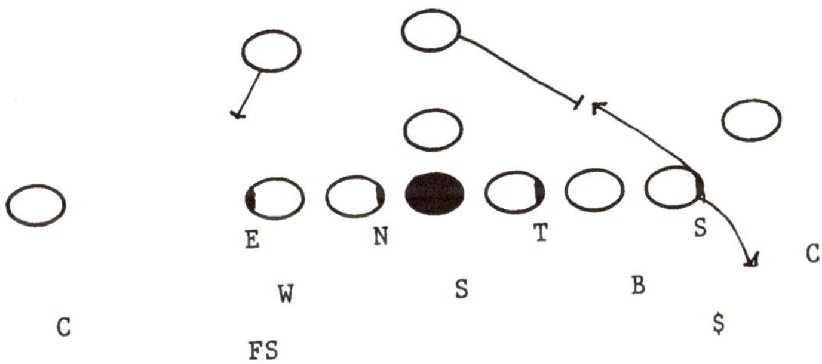

DIAGRAM 5-3
Pass Rush

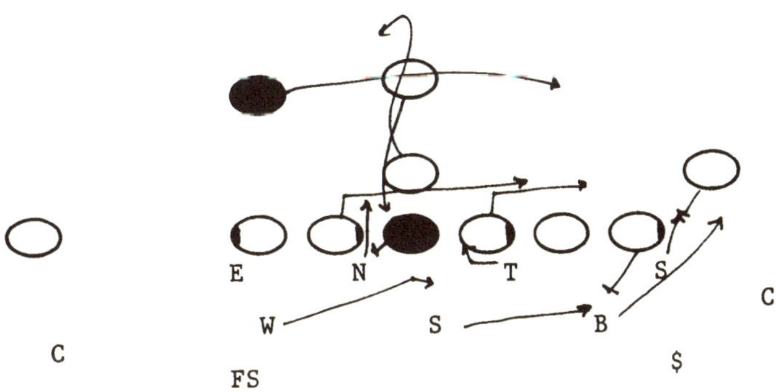

DIAGRAM 5-4
Sweep

If the end gets an inside release with the fullback away, he starts upfield expecting sweep, but if the wing doesn't block him, he then knows it is the waggle. See Diagram 5-5.

The end defeats the tailback's block and rushes the QB. However, if the tailback is accelerating in this area and is not settling to pass block, the end tackles him to help on the throw back to the tailback off waggle action. We tell the officials before the game that we are going to tackle the backs if we are not sure whether they have the ball or not. The QB has just faked to the tailback so he will be tackled. If it is a screen to the tailback, Bandit should make the play; that is his responsibility on the waggle.

If the tight end blocks down and the fullback is to the Stud, the end should think power or G scheme. He should squeeze the off-tackle area and wrong arm any blocker. See Diagrams 5-6 and 5-7.

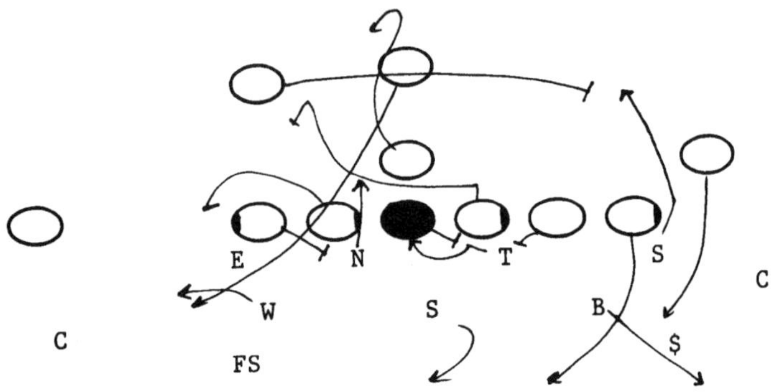

DIAGRAM 5-5
Waggle

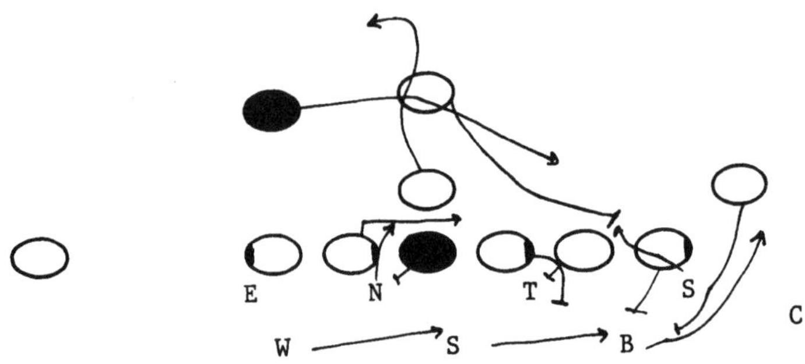

DIAGRAM 5-6
Power

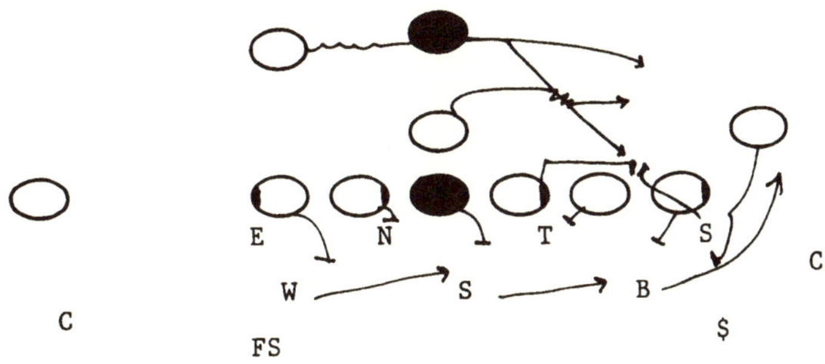

DIAGRAM 5-7
G Scheme

THE 5 TECHNIQUE'S PLAY

The technique involved in coaching the 5 technique is a little more complicated than that used by the chew end, but it is a direct carryover from our normal base end play.

We prioritize our reads to the open end. Versus a down block by the offensive tackle, we use the following progression, which is illustrated in Diagram 5-8:

- #1 Pin by onside guard
- #2 Bootleg-kickout
- #3 Load
- #4 QB

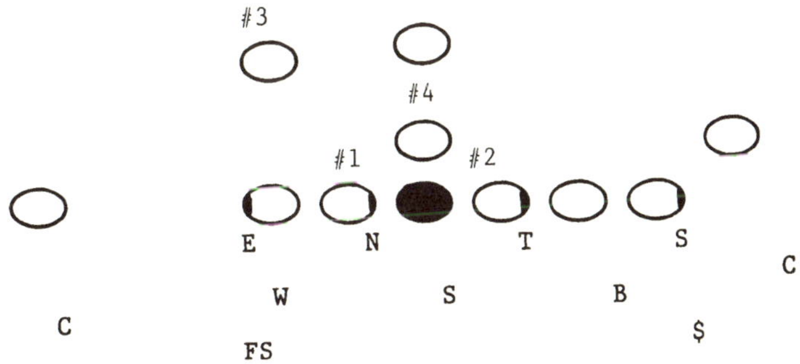

DIAGRAM 5-8
Key Progression

Reads 1 and 2 can be read on the end's first step. Eyes are important in any scheme and especially so versus the Wing-T. Again, our end is in a two-point stance, which helps his vision.

From a two-point stance, the end keys the onside guard through the tackle. If the guard flashes, he gets upfield and eats up the guard's block and the off guard's block. We must get the QB pulled up on the waggle. See Diagram 5-9.

If the offside guard is getting depth in the pull lane, the end must get upfield to get the QB pulled up. If the QB isn't much of a run threat, the end can two gap or play down the middle of the guard. See Diagram 5-10.

If the offside guard is coming flat out of the pull lane, the end does not get depth but instead attacks the guard with a far-shoulder technique. This will make the criss cross bounce. See Diagram 5-11.

The end should be able to read a pin, waggle, or criss-cross scheme on his first step and first look. These blocks will come out of the pull lane.

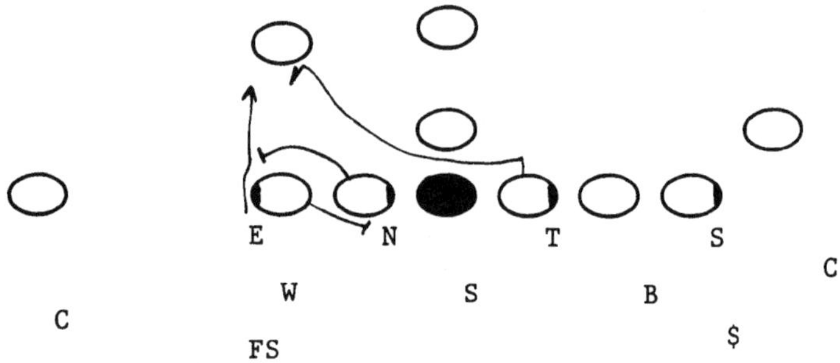

DIAGRAM 5-9
Pin Block

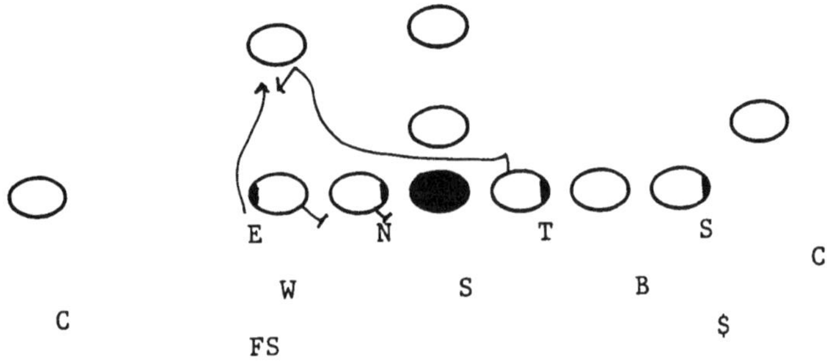

DIAGRAM 5-10
Solid Waggle Scheme

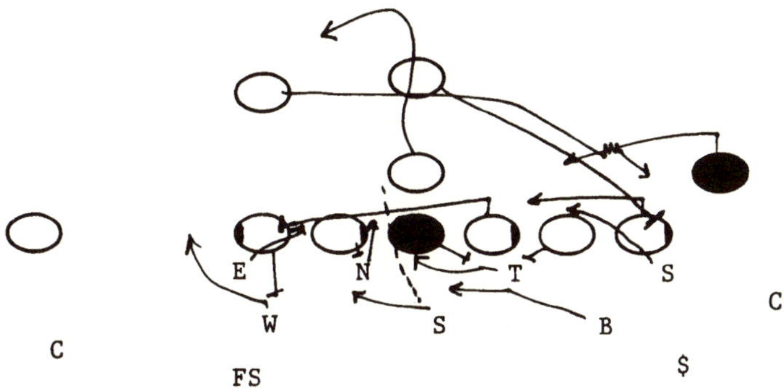

DIAGRAM 5-11
Criss Cross

If the end gets nothing out of the pull lane, his eyes go to the onside back. If the back threatens his outside, he gets upfield to attack this threat. The end must keep outside leverage.

If the end gets nothing out of the pull lane and the back is away, he goes upfield and searches the QB. He tries to keep the QB on his inside shoulder.

STUD'S PLAY VS. RED MOTION

Whenever the wing goes in motion, the corner to that side gives a "Red, Red" call. This "Red" call changes Stud's read. His eyes now go from the fullback to the QB. If the Stud sees the QB's face, he thinks red waggle. The end drives upfield, which makes it impossible for the onside guard to pin him. The end pulls up the QB and allows Bandit a good opportunity to sack the QB on his run-through. See Diagram 5-12.

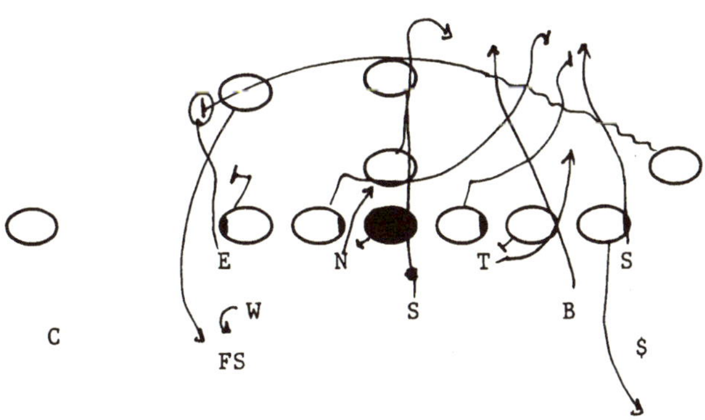

DIAGRAM 5-12
Red Waggle

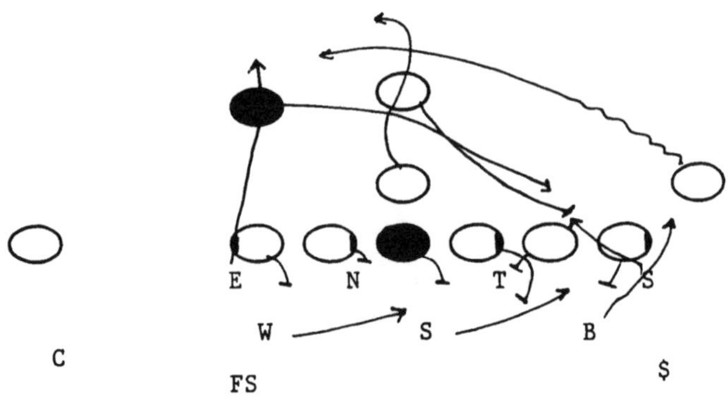

DIAGRAM 5-13
Power Play

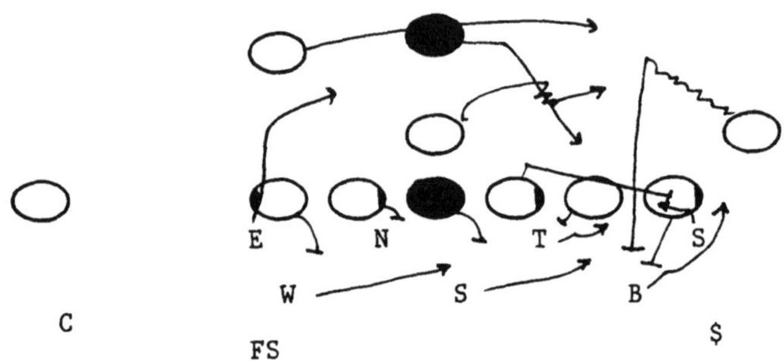

DIAGRAM 5-14
G Lead

If the play is the red trap or sweep, the Stud continues upfield searching the QB and goes to the ball late.

If the Stud sees the QB's back, he will close for a power play or G lead. See Diagrams 5-13 and 5-14.

THE 5 TECHNIQUE VS. RED MOTION

The 5-technique end will take his eyes to the tailback when he hears the "Red" call. The tailback now is the read. The end should feel the tackle but key the back. If the tailback is in the cheat or slot position, the end should drop his outside foot back, which opens him to the back. This allows the end to see the back more clearly and allows the end to tight cross-face the back or hold leverage, depending on the game plan for that week.

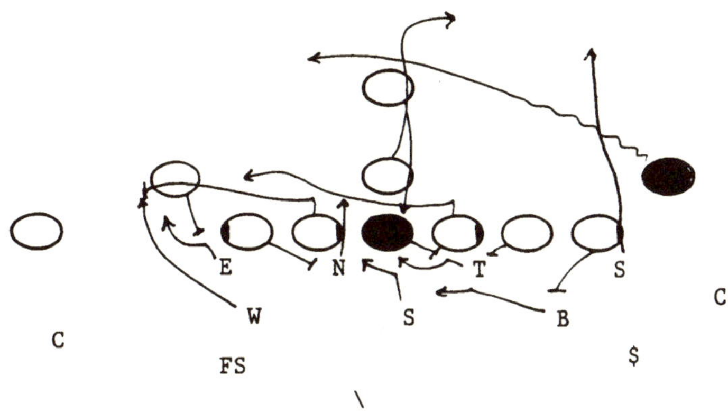

DIAGRAM 5-15
Red Sweep

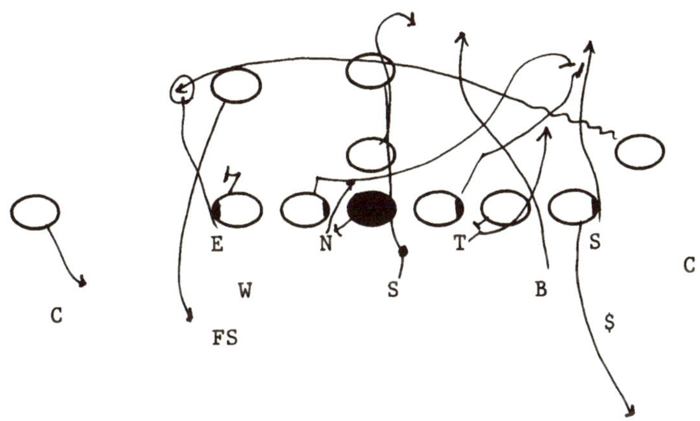

DIAGRAM 5-16
Red Waggle

If the tailback blocks or threatens the end's outside shoulder, the end will lock out and tight cross-face the back's block. See Diagram 5-15.

When the end cross-faces the tailback's block, there is a crease between the end and the nose. A back with good cutting ability can gash the defense in that area. Another way to play this block is to hold leverage with the end. This eliminates the cutback. We have gone into games with the ability to play both ways. Will must decide whether to fit in over the top of the end, or he may go under the block. When the scheme is to hold leverage, Will fits in over the top. Option off red motion can be played the same way.

Whenever the back steps around to the B gap or attacks the B gap from the tailback position, the end will get a base block from the tackle. The end should hold leverage and not run around the tackle's block. In some cases we will cross-face the turnout block and make the isolation bounce.

If the key releases outside and the end gets a pass set by the tackle, the end has screen responsibility. See Diagram 5-16.

6

Secondary Play

The coverage presented here is man coverage. In our terminology we call it Cover 1 Tailback. We had five interceptions in the 1999 State Championship game using this coverage. We have found that man coverage always allows us to get body on body. With man coverage we eliminate seams and avoid guarding grass. Teams that seek to stretch the defense horizontally or vertically versus zone coverages are ineffective. The philosophy of attacking the coverage by high-lowing a defender is nullified. Regardless of whether an opponent's passing attack is predicated on action passes away from the flow, action passes toward the flow, drop-back, or sprint-out passes, we will always get body on body. Versus the basic pass pattern in the Wing-T system, the waggle, we will always have a double team on the fullback and the tight end. If teams choose to attack the defense with the red waggle, we will have a double team on the tight end and the tailback. The fullback can be eliminated from the route by the Sam linebacker.

A major key to successfully defending the Wing-T pass game is to get the QB pulled up quickly. The ends, through their techniques, will get this done. In this scheme it would be beneficial to flip-flop corners. The best cover man should be to the split-end side. Most teams will put their best receiver in this slot. The corner must be able to play this receiver man to man with no help most of the time. The corner to the wing/tight-end side obviously should be a better run player.

SECONDARY ALIGNMENT

The weak corner's vertical depth is determined by ability. Horizontally the corner must align inside because he probably will not have any post help. The corner will key the three-step drop to #1. On runs to him, he is a secondary support player, and on runs away, he is cutoff.

The strong corner's alignment is 5 to 6 yards deep with an outside shade. The corner will key the wing/tight-end area. He is responsible for the wing but must peripherally see the tight end. When the corner gets a down block on the end, he supports the run. If the wing is upfield at all, the corner must honor pass.

The strong safety's alignment is 8 yards over the tight end, and he keys the wing/tight-end area. The reason for peripherally seeing the wing is that a down block by the tight end to the linebacker might be confused as a pass release. The safety may have a seed of doubt as to what the tight end is doing. With the down block by the wing, the safety knows it is a running play. Versus a pass release, the safety will take the tight end man to man. His responsibility versus a running play is to fill where needed.

The free safety's alignment is 8 yards deep over the tailback. The free safety will key the fullback/tailback area and underkey the weak guard. If the backs split with the guard away, the safety plays from the trap to sweep. With both backs away, the safety will eyeball the tight-end/wing area for any reverse or counter coming back. If the play is away, the safety will play his normal B gap to fold technique. If the backs divide and the guard is to the safety or the fullback is wider, the safety will take the fullback in the flat with Will providing underneath coverage on the waggle.

SECONDARY PLAY VS. THE 20 SERIES

The weak corner will play three-step drop to cutoff. The strong corner will support. The strong safety will fill where needed, and the free safety has trap to sweep responsibility. See Diagram 6-1.

Versus the waggle, the weak corner is man on #1 weak. He keys the three-step drop to #1. The receiver can run a flag, post corner, out, or sideline. The corner has him man to man with no help.

The strong corner has the wing man. The strong safety will take the tight end on the drag with Sam supplying underneath coverage. The free safety has the fullback in the flat with Will under the fullback. See Diagram 6-2.

SECONDARY PLAY VS. THE 30 SERIES

Versus the 30 series sweep, the weak corner keys the three-step drop to cutoff. The strong corner supplies support when the wing blocks down on the end. The strong safety will fill where needed. The

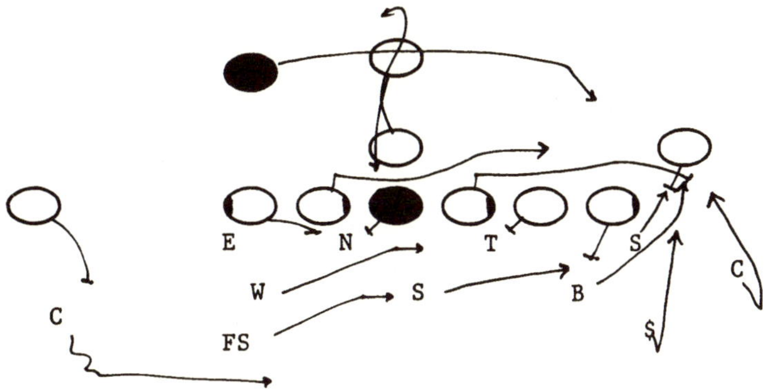

DIAGRAM 6-1
Secondary Play vs. Buck Sweep

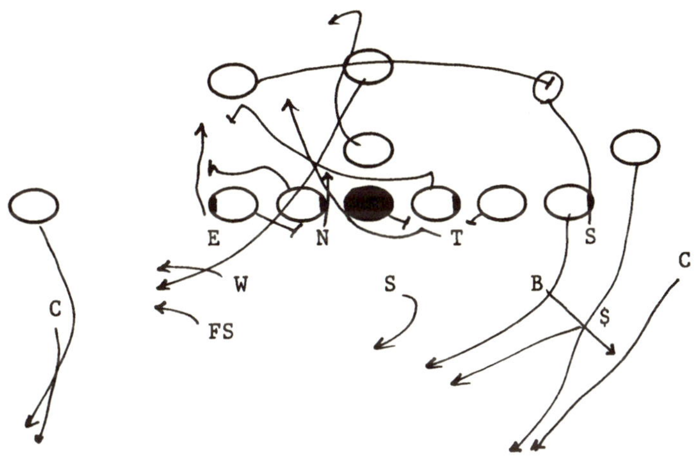

DIAGRAM 6-2
Secondary Play vs. the Waggle

free safety will key the wing/tight end when both backs go away for reverses and counters, then will play B gap to fold. See Diagram 6-3.

Against the 30 series counter criss cross, the weak corner keys the three-step drop to late second contain. The strong corner calls counter and hangs for a play out the front door to cutoff.

The free safety reads both backs away and will vision the wing/tight-end area. He will see both the tight end and the wing come back to him. The safety will attack and stack behind the end and be able to play the bounce out or fall inside.

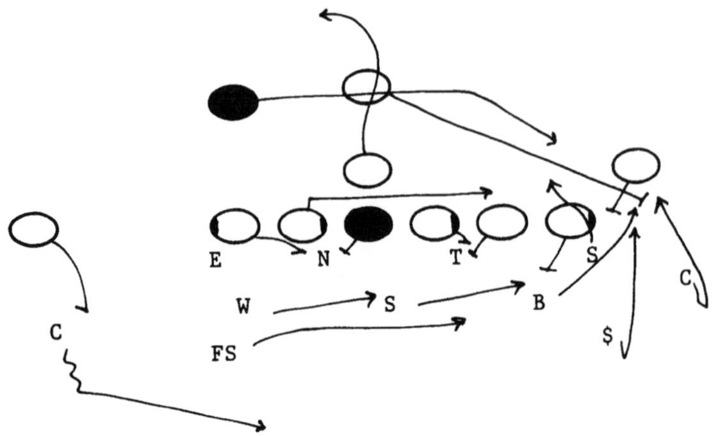

DIAGRAM 6-3
Power Sweep

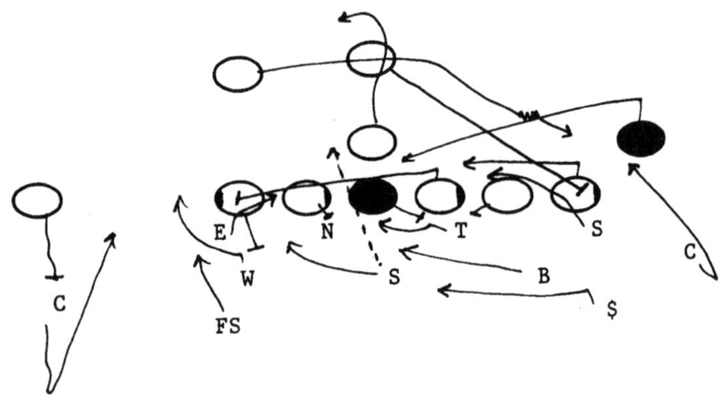

DIAGRAM 6-4
Counter Criss Cross

The strong safety's key pulls to the weak side. The safety will attack the counter hole. See Diagram 6-4.

SECONDARY PLAY VS. THE STRONGSIDE BELLY SERIES

Versus the G scheme off the belly series, the weak corner keys the three-step drop to cutoff. The strong corner's key, the wing, is upfield trying to influence the end. This will cause the corner to be a little soft. The strong safety will also be soft initially because he does not get an immediate block from either the wing or the tight end. The Bandit has force. The corner and the strong safety will step up when they read run. The free safety will see both backs away. This takes his focus to the tight-end/wing area. On this play the free safety will have gap to fold. See Diagram 6-5.

Against the belly down option, the weak corner again keys the three-step drop to cutoff. The strong corner will be soft as he reads the wing who is influencing the Stud. The Bandit will be over the top of the wing and will force the QB to pitch the ball. The corner will take the pitch. The strong safety's keys are upfield so the safety will be soft at first, then he will play inside out to the pitch. The free safety will see both backs away, which will send him from B gap to fold. See Diagram 6-6.

Versus the Sally play, the weak corner will key the three-step drop to cutoff. When the strong corner's key goes away, he should

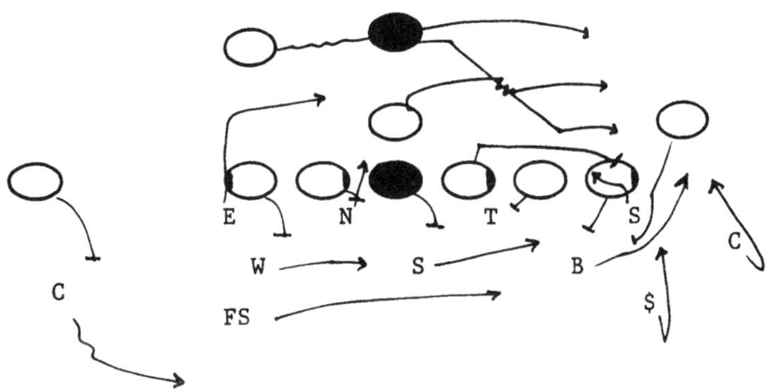

DIAGRAM 6-5
Belly G Scheme

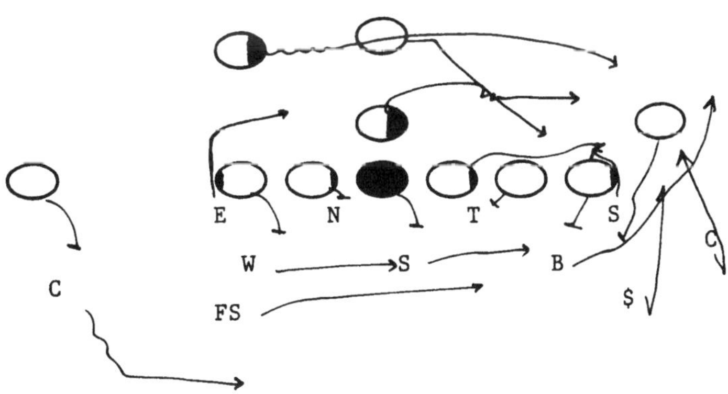

DIAGRAM 6-6
Belly Down Option

hang and look for something coming out the front door. The strong safety's key bases the end. The safety will attack and look inside for the ball. With both backs away, the free safety will key the wing area. With the wing coming back, the free safety will step up to make the play. See Diagram 6-7.

Versus the belly keep pass, the weak corner will take #1 man. The strong corner will get a pass release by both the wing and the tight end. He should take the wing man to man. The strong safety will get the same read as the corner. He should take the tight end man. The free safety will see both backs leave, and the ball will leave the LOS. He should gain depth and look for crossers. See Diagram 6-8.

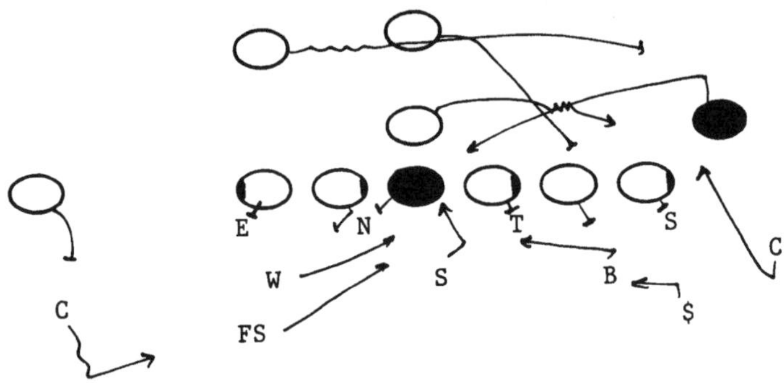

DIAGRAM 6-7
Sally

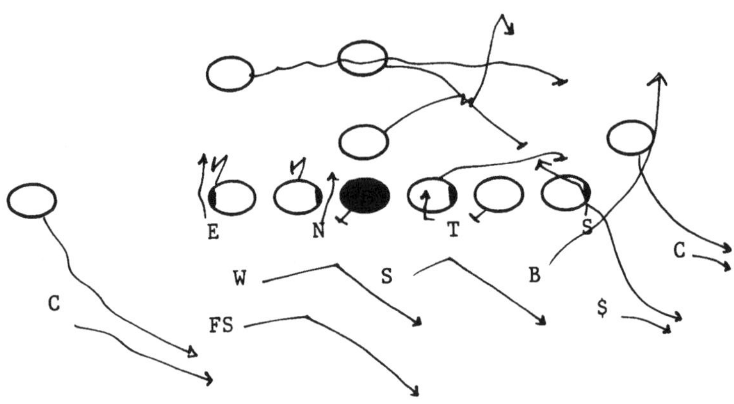

DIAGRAM 6-8
Belly Keep Pass

SECONDARY PLAY VS. RED MOTION

The strong corner will give a "Red" call whenever the wing motions away. He will call red versus deep wing motion or flat wing motion. Versus flat red motion, the corner will give the Sam a "Gone" call and follow the receiver across the formation. This signals Sam that he has the fullback by himself on the red waggle.

The strong corner will loosen and widen if the wing goes on deep red motion. The corner will key the guard to his side. See Diagram 6-9.

If the guard pulls to him, the corner helps Sam with the fullback on the fullback's flat route. If Sam has eliminated the fullback, the corner sinks to give the strong safety underneath help on a flag route. See Diagrams 6-10 and 6-11.

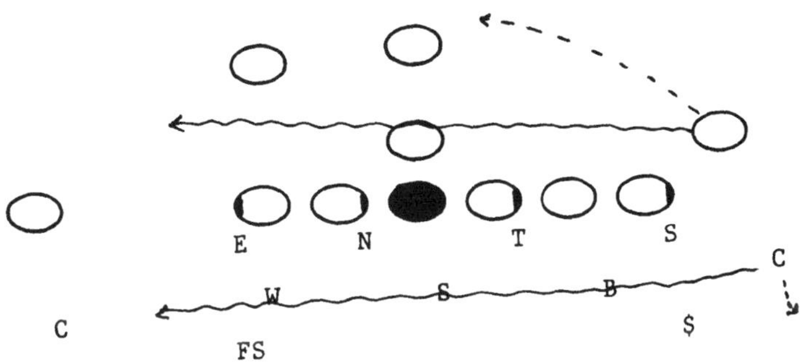

DIAGRAM 6-9
Red Motion

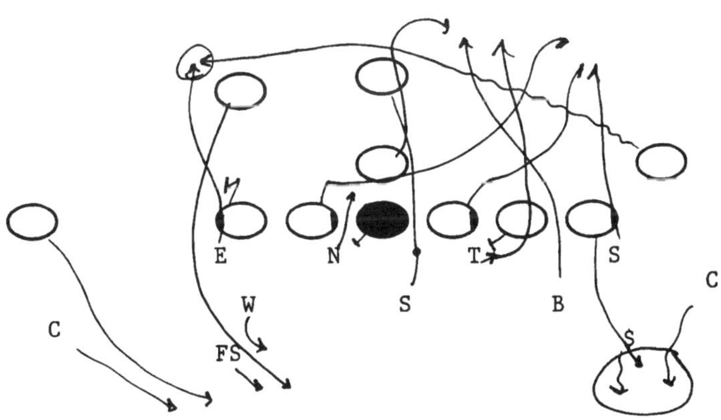

DIAGRAM 6-10
Red Waggle — Fullback Eliminated

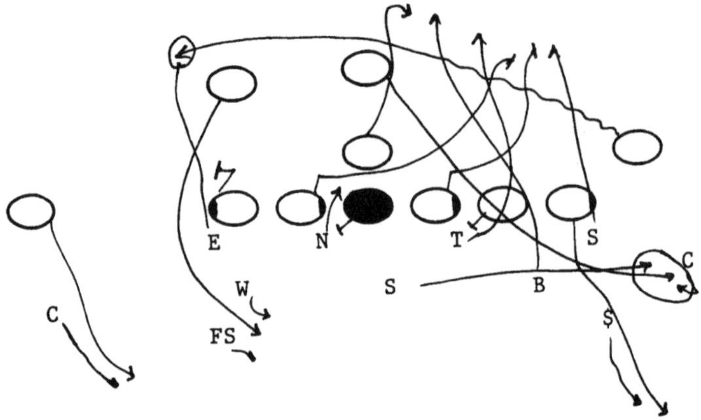

DIAGRAM 6-11
Red Waggle — Fullback in Route

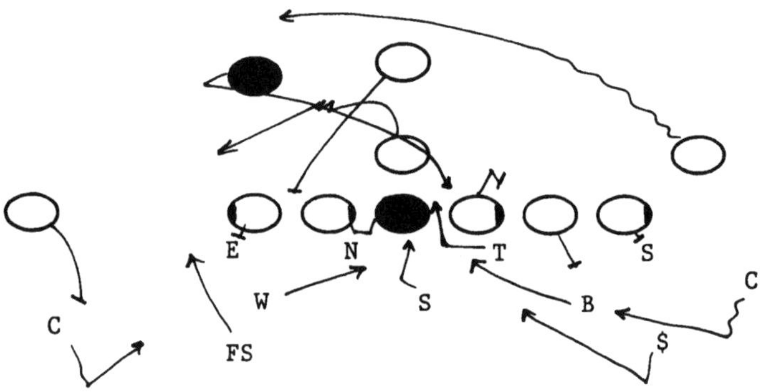

DIAGRAM 6-12
Sally

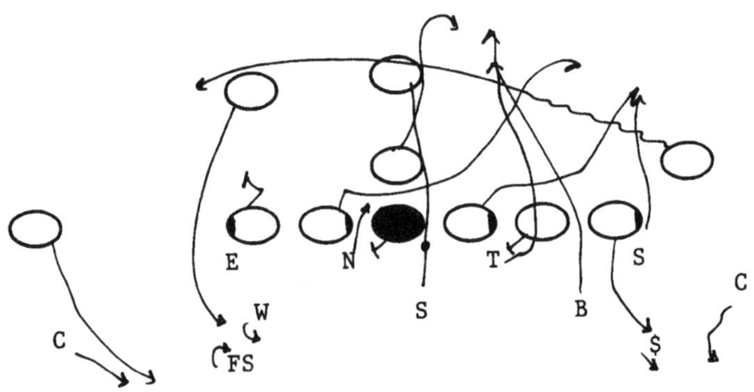

DIAGRAM 6-13
Guard to Strong Safety

If the guard pulls away from the corner, he thinks trap-sweep-counter to cutoff. When the guard pass sets, the corner will fill to help on the Sally play. See Diagram 6-12.

The strong safety will echo the "Red" call. The call must get across the defense to Will and the free safety. The safety feels the strong guard and keys the tight end. With the guard pulling to the safety, the tight end will possibly be on a pass route. He should take the tight end man. See Diagram 6-13.

If the guard pulls away, the safety keys the tight end and plays from trap to sweep, B gap to fold. If the guard pass sets or down blocks, the safety attacks the LOS on his side of the ball for counter.

When the free safety gets the "Red" call, he keys the tailback. If the tailback blocks the end, the safety will support. See Diagrams 6-14 and 6-15.

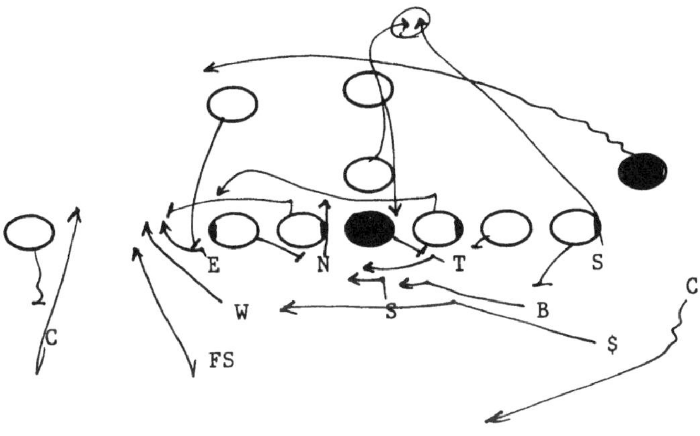

DIAGRAM 6-14
Sweep

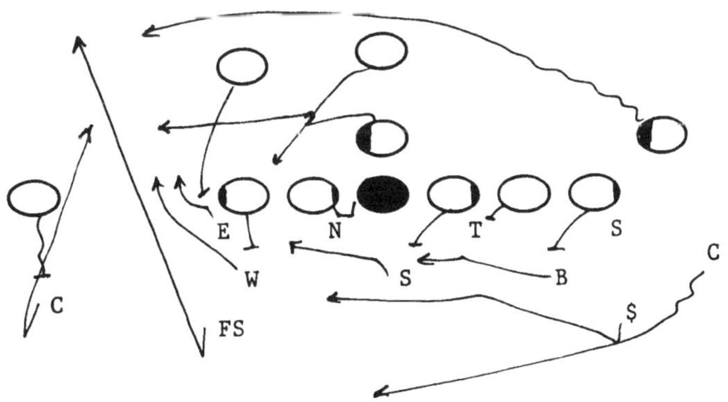

DIAGRAM 6-15
Option

If the tailback leads or folds inside on Will, the free safety will go to a stack position and be able to help inside or outside on the isolation. See Diagram 6-16.

If the tailback counter steps, the safety must feel the fullback. If the fullback is sifting his way through, the safety will take him on the tackle trap boot. If the fullback blocks, the safety will fall inside to help on the counter. See Diagram 6-17.

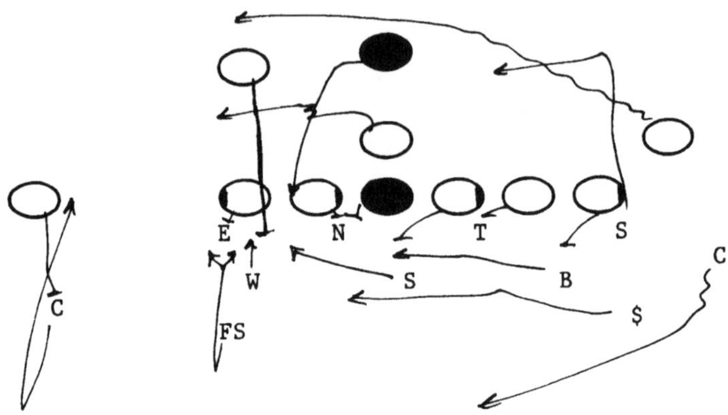

DIAGRAM 6-16
Isolation

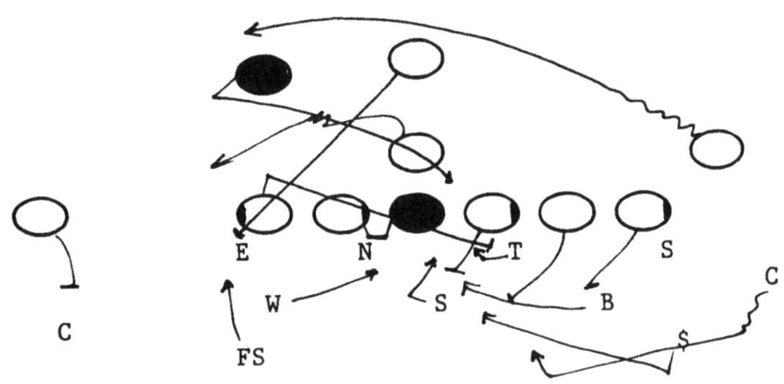

DIAGRAM 6-17
Tackle Trap

If the tailback releases to the flat immediately, the free safety will jump him. The Will linebacker has underneath coverage. See Diagram 6-18.

On the red waggle, the tailback will probably run a drag. The free safety will cover him man, with Will providing help underneath. See Diagram 6-19.

The weak corner keys the three-step drop to #1. On run plays to the corner, he has secondary support. On plays away, the corner has cutoff. Versus pass, the weak corner has #1 man.

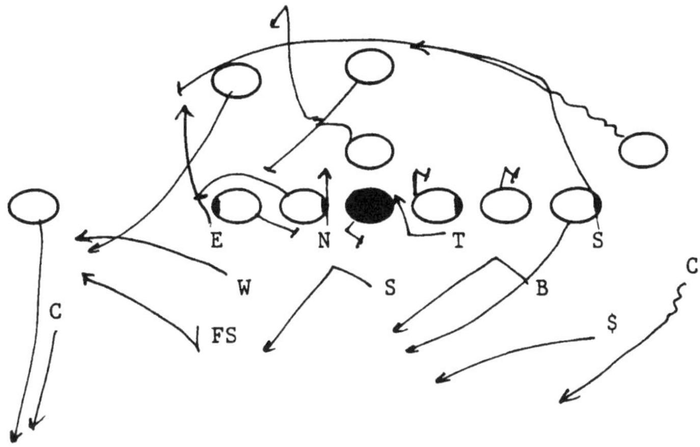

DIAGRAM 6-18
Belly Keep Pass

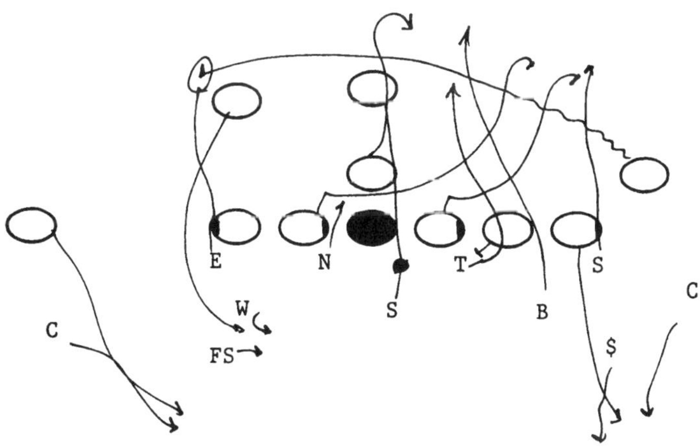

DIAGRAM 6-19
Red Waggle

7

Formations, Wheels, and Motions

This chapter deals with how to successfully counter one of the Wing-T's major strengths. Chapter 7 shows how the defense can adjust to and defeat the myriad ways the Wing-T seeks to confuse defenders with its movement package.

SHIFTS

Many teams run the Wing-T because it gives them the flexibility to align in a variety of formations. If a team has the concept that a back can be a wing, or a wing can be a back, it can cause the defense recognition problems. Add to this the Wing-T's mix of formations, slide to's, shift to's, and jump to's with motion, and the multitude of problems increases. To combat these, the defense must have in place a simple but flexible system. We feel we have that system. To keep our reads and keys consistent, we must identify the potential red motion player. Normally the declaration of the front will be to the wing/tight-end side of the formation. However, with the Wing-T movement package and multiple formations, this can be difficult but not impossible. Recognition periods are a must in a defensive team's preparation time for a Wing-T opponent.

Diagrams 7-1(a) through 7-1(f) illustrate basic formations and strength declarations. The red motion man is highlighted. Balanced formations are declared to our left, regardless of hash considerations. We do this because we keep it consistent and most teams are right-handed. In our defense Bandit and the strong safety go together, and

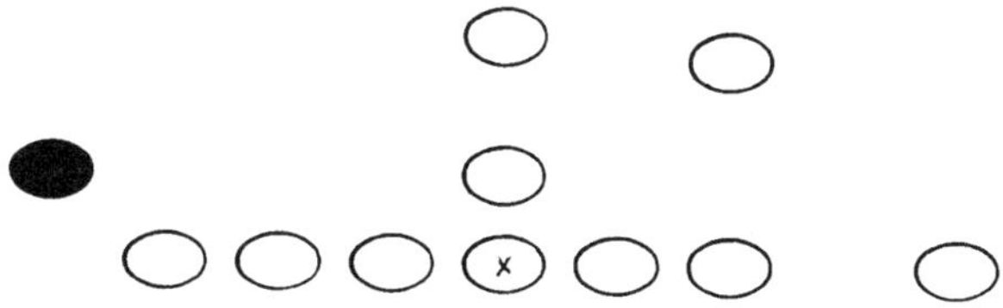

DIAGRAM 7-1(a)
Formations — Wing Left

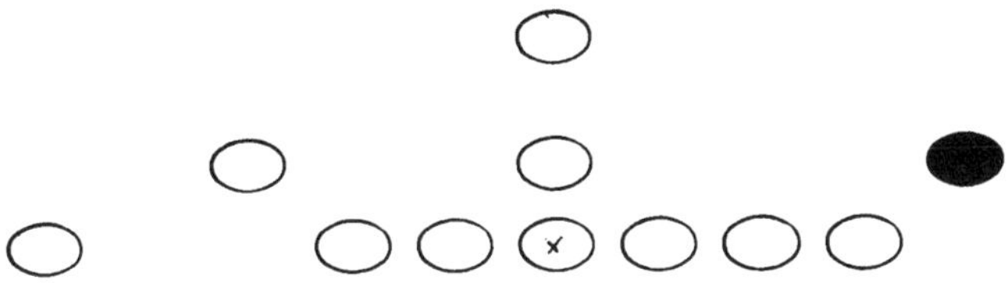

DIAGRAM 7-1(b)
Formations — Wing-Right Cheat

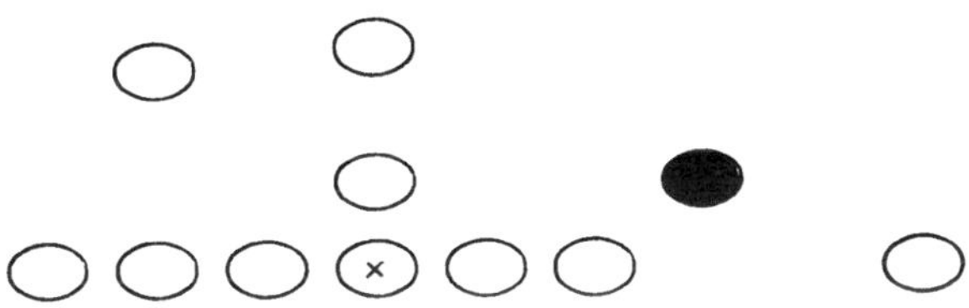

DIAGRAM 7-1(c)
Formations — Slot Right

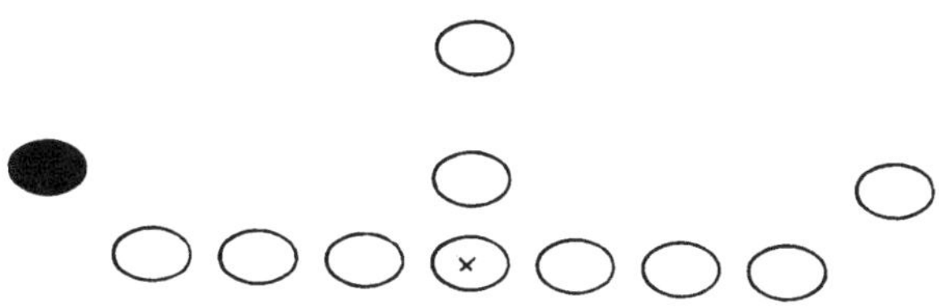

DIAGRAM 7-1(d)
Formations — Double Wing

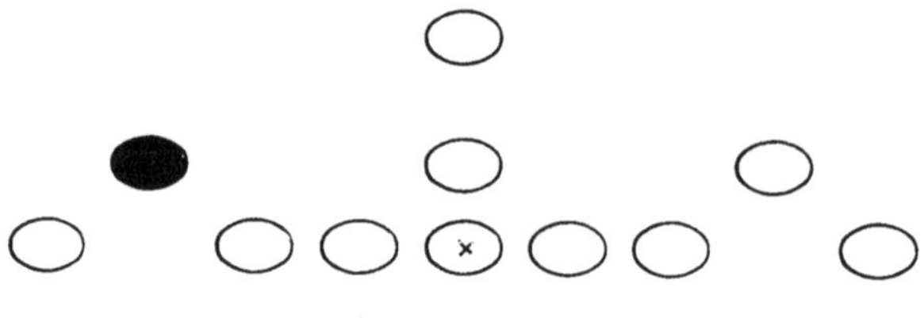

DIAGRAM 7-1(e)
Formations — Double Slot

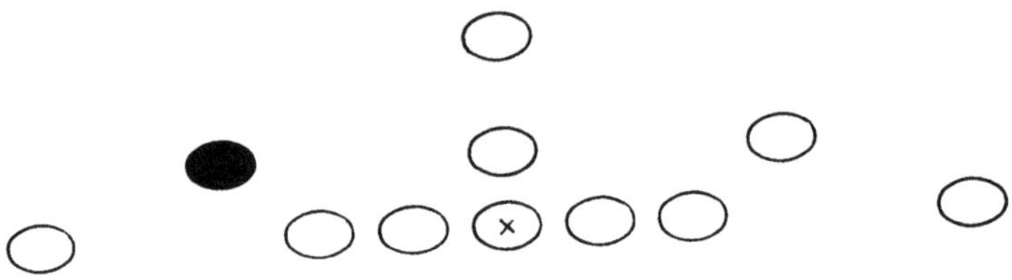

DIAGRAM 7-1(f)
Formations — Mirror

Will is teamed with the free safety. Once we have made our declaration, we have tabbed the potential red motion player.

Diagram 7-2 illustrates the trade from wing left to end over right. In this situation we make an "Omaha" call and flip to a new strength call. This becomes a "Rip." In most cases we will bring the corner over and run a crash with him.

Diagram 7-3 illustrates the wing left slide to slot right. To explain this movement, we simply say the wing red motioned to the halfback position. So in essence the offense didn't change formations—they just went in red motion. The formation is simply a wing-left cheat with red motion.

When this happens we call "Red, Red" and go to our red motion keys. Diagrams 7-4 and 7-5 show two plays from this "slide-to" look to illustrate how we would play it.

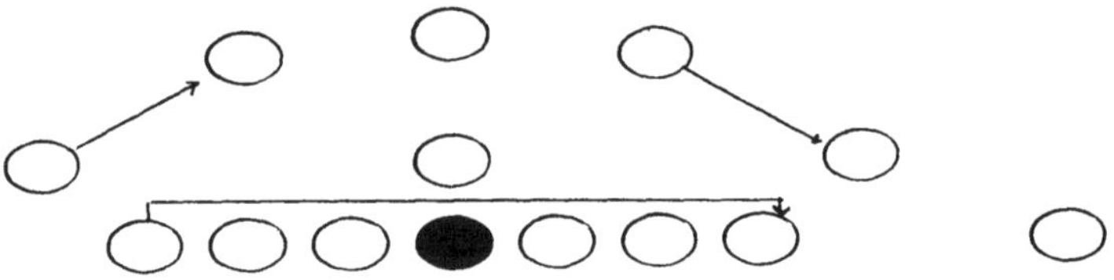

DIAGRAM 7-2
Trade From Wing Left to End Over Right

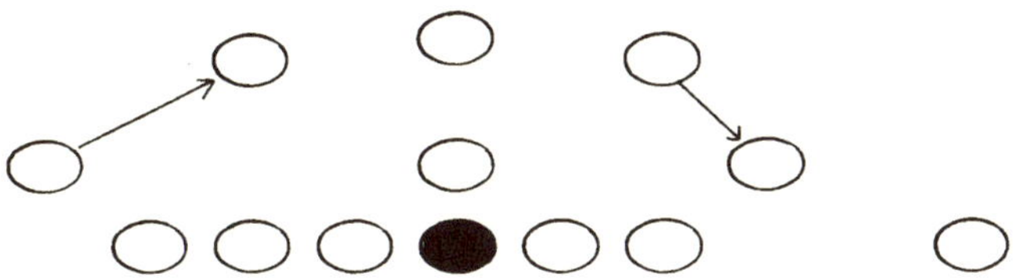

DIAGRAM 7-3
Slide to: Wing Left to Slot Right

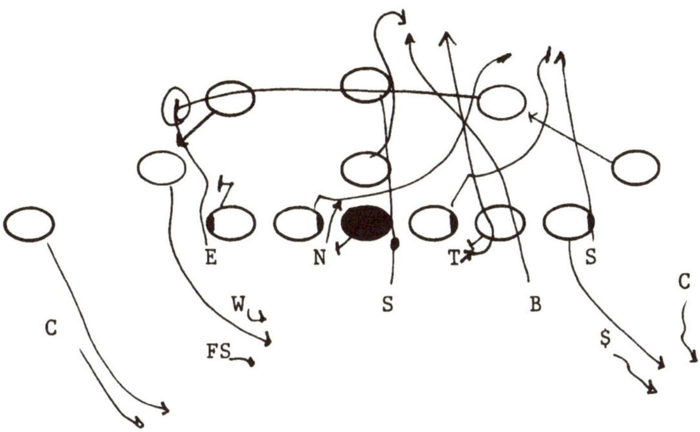

DIAGRAM 7-4
Red Waggle

By position, we would play the red waggle as follows (see Diagram 7-4):

Tackle—Plays trap first. When he feels the down block by the tackle, he backdoors or cross-faces to the QB.

Nose—Penetrates backdoor to the QB.

Stud—With "Red" call, keys the QB. The QB's face will show, so the Stud gets upfield to pull up the QB.

End—His eyes go to the tailback with the "Red" call. The tailback's pass release will cause the end to step out, then read the tackle's pass block. The end has screen responsibility on the halfback.

Bandit—His red motion key is the onside guard. The guard pulls to Bandit. This sends Bandit on a run-through to the QB.

Sam—His red motion key is the fullback. If the fullback is down the midline, he tackles him. This will eliminate him from the route. If the fullback is wider, Sam must gain width and take him in the flat.

Will—With red motion, he visions the tailback. If the tailback is upfield, Will walls his inside shoulder, man turns on him, and plays man under coverage.

Strong Corner—When the wing moves to the halfback position, the corner will give a "Red, Red" call, loosen, and key the strong guard. On the red waggle, the guard will pull to the corner. The strong corner will look to help Sam with the fullback in the flat. If Sam has eliminated the fullback, the corner will get depth to help the strong safety on the tight end.

Strong Safety—With a "Red" call from the strong corner, the safety feels the strong guard and keys the tight end. With the guard pulling to the safety and the tight end upfield, the safety knows he is facing the red waggle. He will take the tight end; underneath help is possible from the corner depending on whether the fullback gets out into his pattern. He will play as if he will get no help.

Free Safety—Versus red motion, he keys the tailback. In this case the tailback will be upfield. The free safety will take him man. He should understand that Will is providing underneath help.

Weak Corner—Keys the three-step drop to #1. The corner will take him man.

By position, we would play the slot to wing: influence trap as follows (see Diagram 7-5):

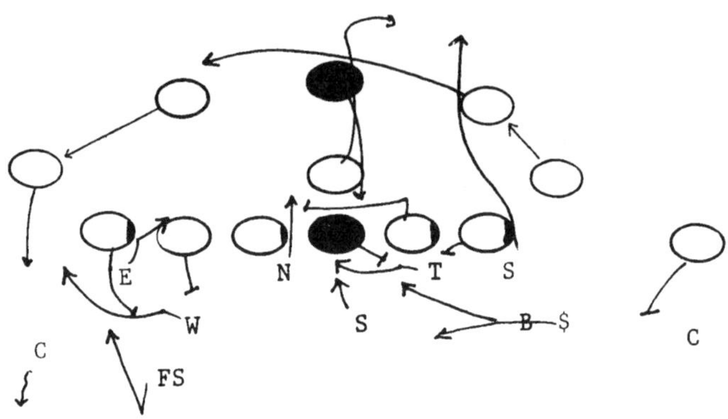

DIAGRAM 7-5
Slot to Wing: Influence Trap

Tackle—Cross-faces the turnback block by the center and gets north.

Nose—Penetrates. On this play the nose will be trapped.

Stud—With the "Red" call, he will key the QB. On this play the Stud will see the QB's face. The Stud's upfield charge serves to search the QB.

End—Anytime the end has a tight end backside, he will move to a 7 technique.

Bandit—Keys the strong guard. When he pulls away, Bandit plays trap to sweep.

Sam—Keys the fullback. With the fullback down the midline, he steps up and makes the tackle. Sam will be unblocked.

Will—Keys the wing. The wing is upfield so Will plays through him for waggle or sweep.

Strong Corner—Keys the wing. With the wing upfield, the corner will have to respect pass.

Weak Corner—Keys the three-step drop to #1. The corner will take him man.

Strong Safety—When the wing shifts, the safety will take his focus to the guard. When the guard pulls away, he will play trap to sweep.

Free Safety—Keys the tight end. With the tight end upfield, he must respect pass.

Some teams will shift from the T formation to a wing set or slot set. We declare to the tight end if faced with this situation. See Diagram 7-6.

The shift to wing, illustrated in Diagram 7-7, presents no problem because they are shifting to the call. All reads and keys are in place.

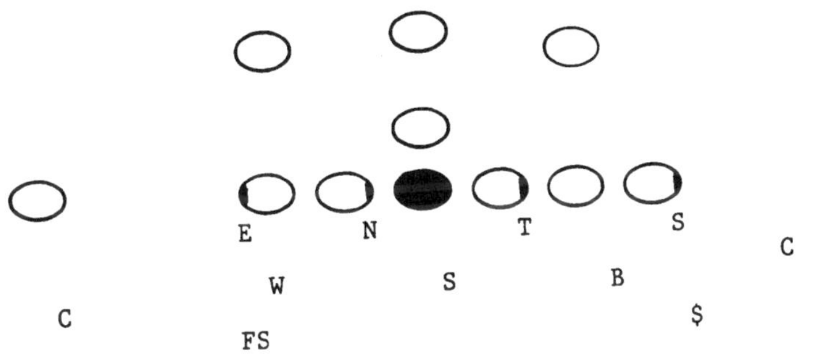

DIAGRAM 7-6
"Rip" Call

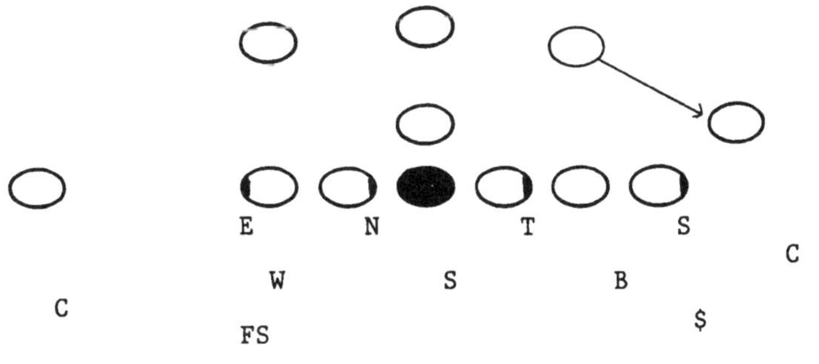

DIAGRAM 7-7
Shift to Wing

The shift to slot, illustrated in Diagram 7-8, can cause major defensive problems unless the defense has a simple and effective adjustment. To keep our keys and reads the same, we simply treat this shift as red motion.

All the offense has done is align in a wing-right cheat formation and sent the wing in red motion.

Diagram 7-9 illustrates how we would play a shift from a T to a slot-left formation.

By position, we would play the 20 series sweep as follows (see Diagram 7-10):

Tackle—Cross-faces the turnback block by the center.

Nose—Penetrates. The right offensive tackle has an uphill block on the play.

Stud—With the "Red" call, the Stud will see the QB's face. On this key he will explode upfield and end up on search on the QB.

End—The end's eyes go to the slot back. When the slot back blocks down on him, he will tight cross-face the block.

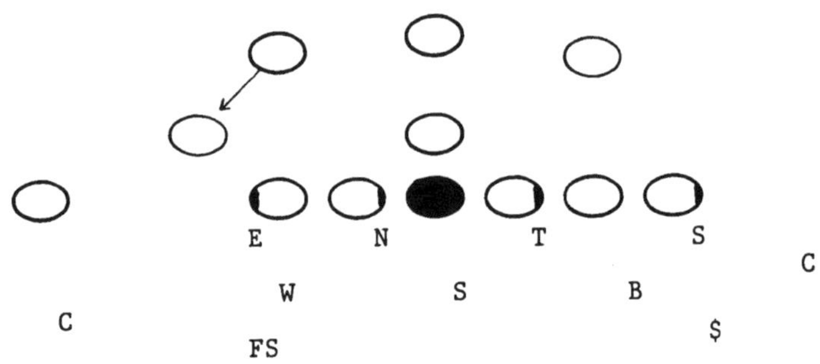

DIAGRAM 7-8
Shift to Slot

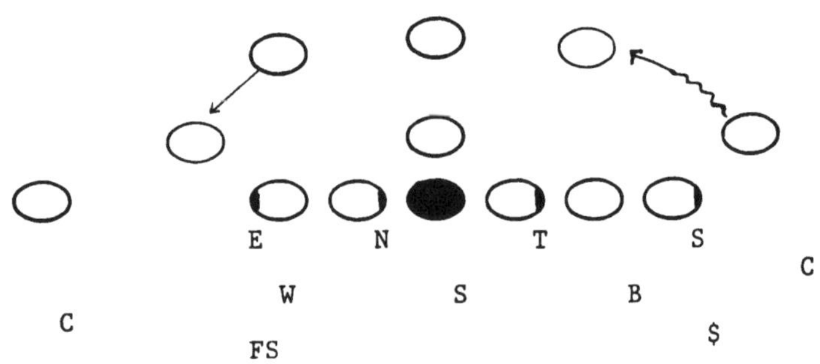

DIAGRAM 7-9
T to Slot

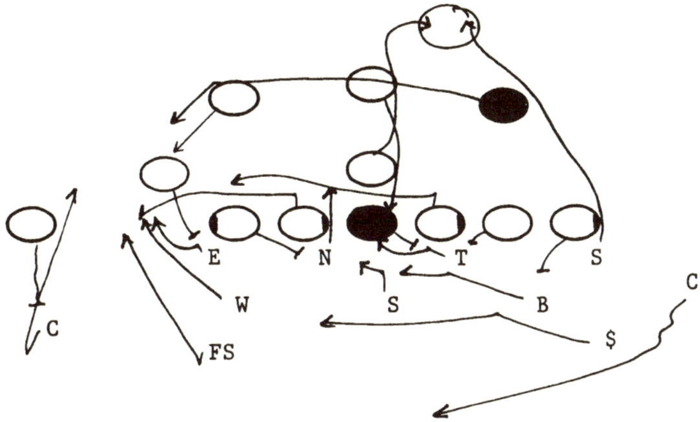

DIAGRAM 7-10
20 Series Sweep

Bandit—Keys the strong guard. When he pulls away, Bandit plays trap to sweep.

Sam—When the fullback is down the midline, Sam plays trap to sweep.

Will—When the slot backs down on the end, Will plays over the top for sweep.

Strong Corner—Keys the guard. When the guard pulls away, the corner thinks trap, sweep, counter to cutoff.

Strong Safety—When the guard pulls away, the safety plays trap to sweep, B gap to fold.

Free Safety—Keys the slot. He forces the sweep when the slot backs down on the end.

Weak Corner—Keys the three-step drop to #1. He will supply secondary support versus sweeps.

The way we play this is to treat the movement as red motion. This keeps our reads and keys the same. The defense does not have to worry about realignment or about players being caught out of position.

MOTIONS

One of the basics to running this defense is identification of the man who would be the initiator of red motion. He must be identified and the front called to his alignment. When he goes in motion, it is a big deal. The defense will make a "Red" call, and we get into the red keys and reads. We look for the tight-end/wing combination first. Balanced formations will be called to the left, regardless of hash considerations.

We distinguish two types of red motion—deep red and flat red.

With deep red motion, illustrated in Diagram 7-11, the strong corner calls "Red, Red" and loosens. The corner's key now is the strong guard. If the "Red" key motions flat across the ball, we call this flat red.

With flat red motion, illustrated in Diagram 7-12, the corner will give Sam a "Gone" call, which tells Sam that he does not have help with the fullback on the red waggle. The strong safety now knows that he will not have any help from the corner on the tight end. All the red keys are the same, regardless of whether the motion is deep or flat. Some teams will motion the wing away from the formation. The only adjustment here is that the corner will widen in his man coverage. All keys and reads are the same.

Some teams will align the wing in a pro set, then motion him back in. We say all he is doing is motioning to his wing position. This

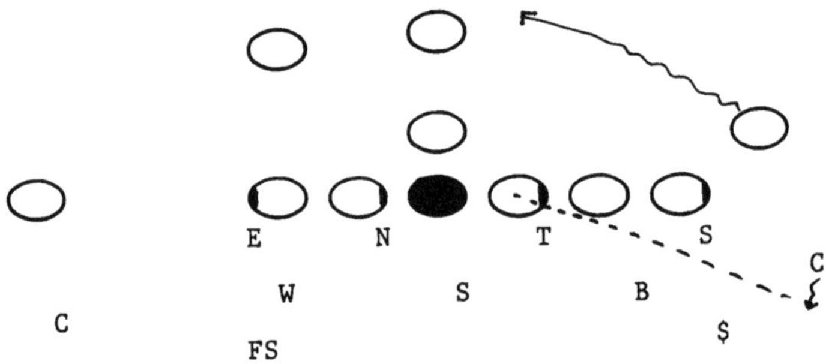

DIAGRAM 7-11
Deep Red Motion

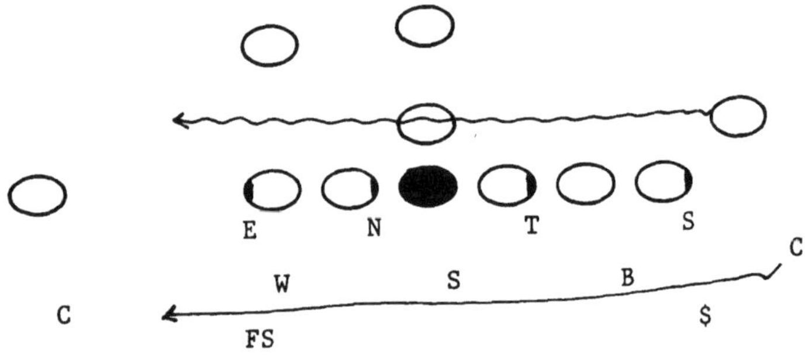

DIAGRAM 7-12
Flat Red Motion

requires no big adjustment unless he gets to the tight end and continues across or goes in deep motion. In this case we make our "Red" call and play accordingly.

The free safety will handle any fullback or tailback motion that leaves the tackle box. This type of motion severely limits the plays that the Wing-T offense can run.

Tailback motion can be confusing unless it is understood that all the back has done is motion to his tailback position. Once we recognize the red motion man, it doesn't matter that the other slot or wing goes in motion. This "blue" motion is to be ignored. See Diagrams 7-13, 7-14, and 7-15.

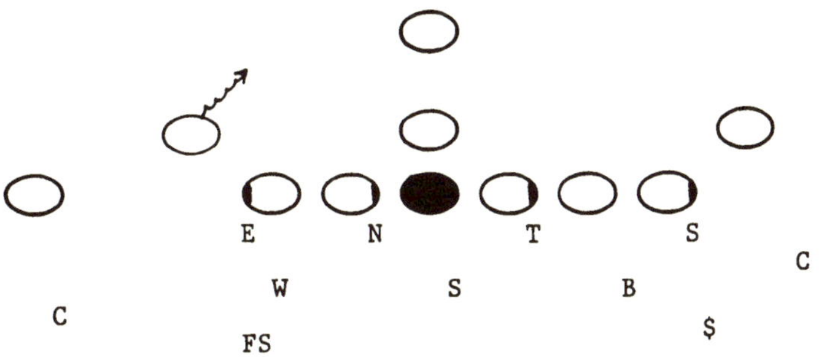

DIAGRAM 7-13
Blue Motion From Wing-Right Cheat

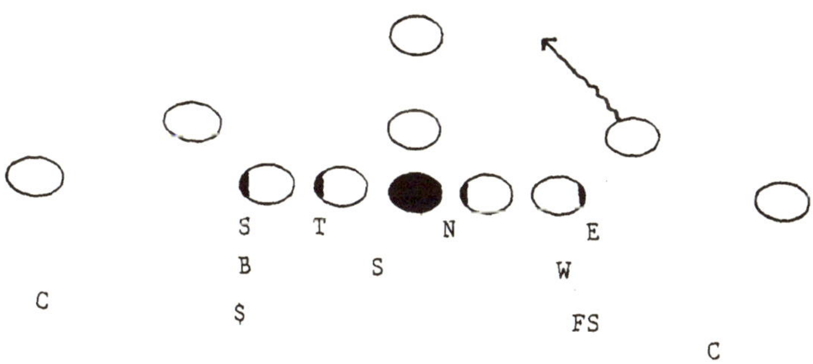

DIAGRAM 7-14
Blue Motion From Mirror

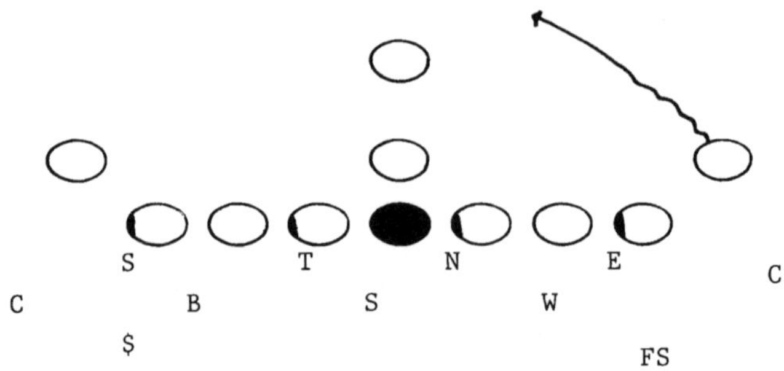

DIAGRAM 7-15
Blue Motion From Double Wing

Remember that balanced formations are declared to the left. Motion by a wing or slot to our right is considered blue motion and does not affect our reads.

8

Attacking the 20 Series

This series is the genesis of the Wing-T system. To successfully attack the Wing-T system, the defense must understand and defeat the 20 series. In this chapter we take the 20 series and show, by position, how we would play it.

DOWN TRAP

By position, we would play the down trap as follows (see Diagram 8-1):

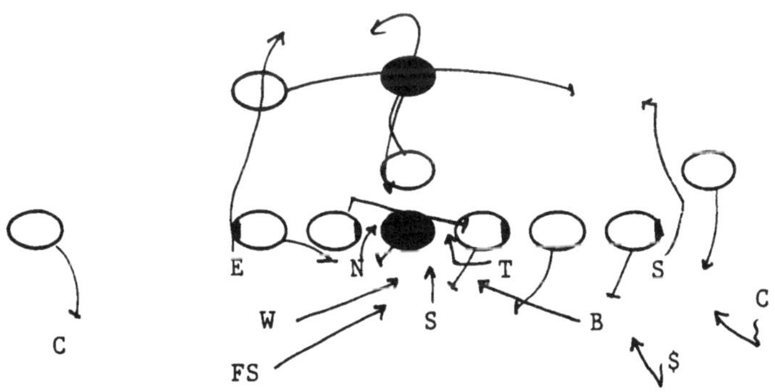

DIAGRAM 8-1
Down Trap

Tackle—Closes and wrong arms the trapper.
Nose—Penetrates and comes backdoor.

Stud—When the fullback is away, this is a sweep read to Stud. He gets upfield and attacks the wing. Should the wing be upfield, the Stud should look inside, find the ball, and use his chase technique.

End—With no pin, no pull-lane threat, and the back away, the end searches the QB.

Bandit—When the fullback is away and the guard is on a down block, Bandit plays trap.

Sam—When the fullback is away and the guard is on a down block, Sam plays trap.

Will—When the fullback is down the midline and the guard is away, Will plays trap.

Weak Corner—Plays man on #1 to cutoff.

Strong Corner—Must respect pass with the wing on an upfield course.

Strong Safety—Must respect pass if the tight end is soft or upfield. If the end bases, the safety must look inside to find the ball.

Free Safety—Gets a divide read with the fullback down the midline. He will play trap to sweep.

The defense will have six men responsible for the down trap.

INFLUENCE TRAP

By position, we would play the influence trap as follows (see Diagram 8-2):

Tackle—Closes and wrong arms the trapper.

Nose—Penetrates and comes backdoor.

Stud—When the fullback is away, this is a sweep read. Stud will get upfield and find the ball when he recognizes that the ball is not in his area.

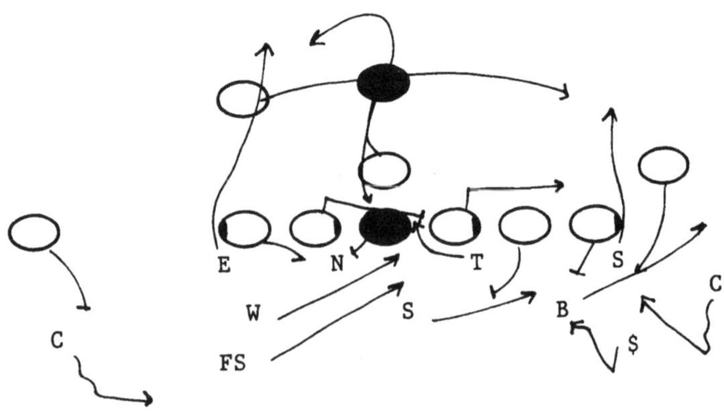

DIAGRAM 8-2
Influence Trap

End—With no pin, no pull-lane threat, and the back away, the end will search the QB.

Bandit—When the fullback is away but the guard pulls to, Bandit plays sweep.

Sam—When the fullback is away but the guard pulls to, Sam plays sweep.

Will—When the fullback is down the midline and the guard is away, Will plays trap.

Weak Corner—Plays man on #1 to cutoff.

Strong Corner—Must respect pass with the wing on an upfield course.

Strong Safety—Must respect pass if the tight end is soft or upfield. If the end bases, the safety must get his eyes inside.

Free Safety—Gets a divide read with the fullback down the midline. He plays trap to sweep.

Versus the influence trap, we will have four defenders with Will unblocked at the POA.

BUCK SWEEP

By position, we would play the buck sweep as follows (see Diagram 8-3):

Tackle—Plays trap first. When he feels the tackle, he goes backdoor or cross-faces.

Nose—Penetrates and backdoors the play.

Stud—With the fullback away, attacks the wing. He makes the back run the hump.

End—With no pin, no pull-lane threat, and the back away, the end will search the QB.

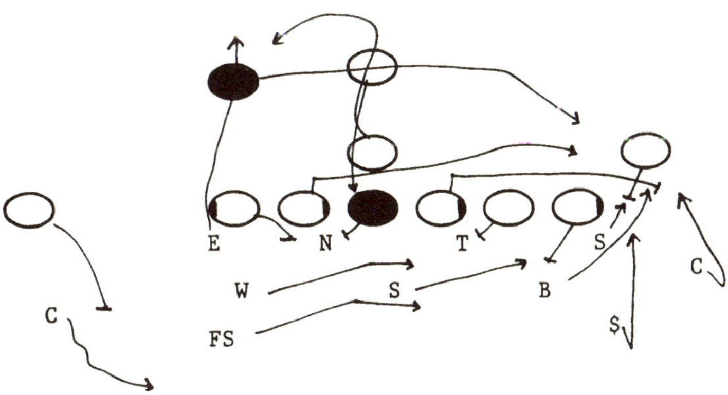

DIAGRAM 8-3
Buck Sweep

Bandit—When the fullback is away but the guard is to him, Bandit plays sweep. Bandit will be the first defender there. He plays the guard down the middle. Bandit must not get kicked out by the guard.

Sam—Plays sweep inside out.

Will—Plays trap to sweep.

Weak Corner—Plays man on #1 to cutoff.

Strong Corner—The down block on Stud by the wing gets him up.

Strong Safety—As he reads the wing area, he will see a definite down block by the wing. The safety will fill where needed.

Free Safety—Plays trap to sweep, B gap to fold.

WAGGLE

By position, we would play the waggle as follows (see Diagram 8-4):

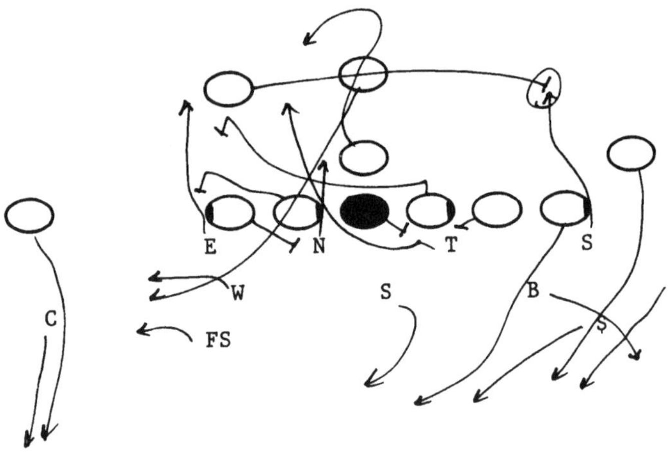

DIAGRAM 8-4
Waggle

Tackle—Tight cross-faces the center's turnback block. He then gets north to the QB.

Nose—Penetrates and beats the tackle's down block.

Stud—When the fullback is away, this is a sweep read. When Stud feels no pressure by the wing, and the tailback is to him in a block mode, Stud will whip his block and rush the QB. If the tailback is motoring in this area, Stud will tackle him or knock him off-course. If he reads screen, he will stick with the tailback.

Bandit—When both the fullback and guard are away, Bandit plays screen or throwback to the tailback.

End—When the tackle blocks down and the guard is in his face, he will explode upfield, use up both guards, and pull the QB up. He must stay on his feet.

Sam—When both the fullback and guard are away, Sam will man turn to the tight end and play him underneath. The strong safety is over the top.

Will—When the fullback and the guard are both to Will, he plays hard under on the fullback. The free safety is over the top. The fullback will probably be wider on the waggle.

Weak Corner—Plays man on #1.

Strong Corner—Plays man on the wing.

Strong Safety—Plays man on the tight end. Sam will assume man under. The safety plays over the top.

Free Safety—Gets a divide read with the fullback wider and the weak guard to. The safety plays over the top of the fullback. Will plays hard underneath coverage on the fullback.

9

Attacking the 30 Series

The second major way Wing-T teams run the sweep is with the power sweep series with the fullback as the lead blocker. Reasons vary as to why teams run this type of sweep. This scheme allows the front side to block solidly if penetration is a problem or if the coach wants to muscle the defense. This series also sets up one of the most devastating plays in football, the counter criss cross.

In this chapter we take the 30 series and show, by position, how we would play it.

POWER SWEEP

By position, we would play the power sweep as follows (see Diagram 9-1):

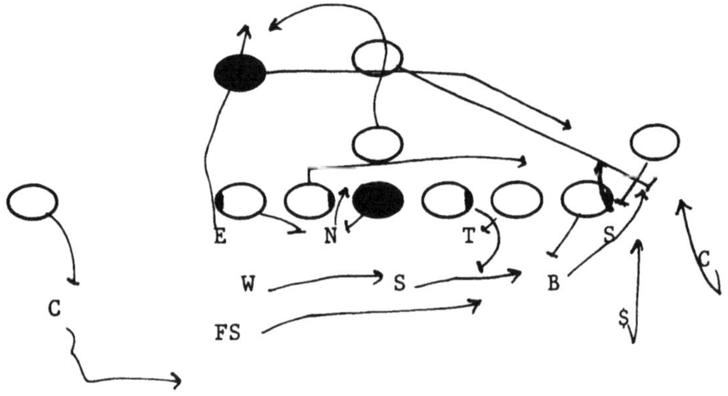

DIAGRAM 9-1
Power Sweep

Tackle—When he feels the tackle's pressure, he comes backdoor or cross-faces when he is sure it is not a trap.

Nose—Penetrates and comes backdoor.

Stud—When the fullback is to him, he thinks power kickout or G scheme. Stud will be down blocked by the wing. He will rally to the ball. We will lose him on this play, but he will make the play on the power kickout or the G scheme.

End—With no pin, no pull-lane threat, and the back away, the end will search the QB.

Bandit—When both the fullback and guard are to him, he plays sweep. Bandit will be the first defender there. Bandit attacks the fullback. Bandit must not get kicked out by the fullback.

Sam—When both the fullback and guard are to Sam, Sam is a sweep player inside out. He checks the wing/tight-end area as he goes.

Will—When the fullback and guard are both away, Will is a sweep player inside out. He checks the wing/tight-end area as he goes.

Weak Corner—Plays man on #1 to cutoff.

Strong Corner—The down block by the wing on Stud gets the corner up.

Strong Safety—As he reads the wing area, he will see a definite down block by the wing. He fills where needed.

Free Safety—With both backs away, he checks the wing area and plays B gap to fold.

CRISS CROSS

By position, we would play the criss cross as follows (see Diagram 9-2):

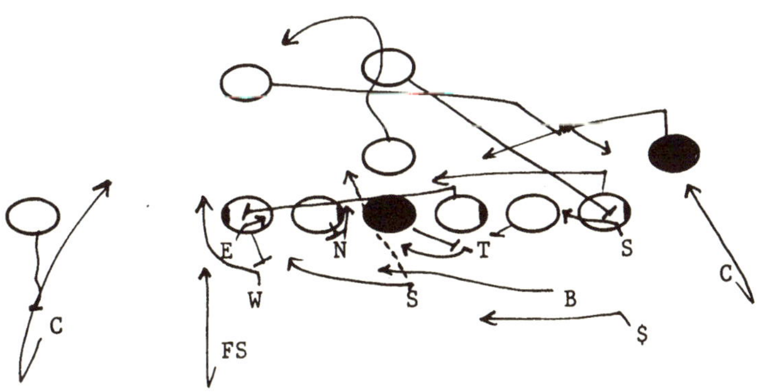

DIAGRAM 9-2
Criss Cross

Tackle—Cross-faces the center's turnback block.

Nose—Penetrates. Penetration will kill this play.

Stud—With the fullback to, he thinks inside. As Stud goes he should feel the tight end pulling away. Stud should flatten and follow him to the POA, trying to get under the fullback's fill block. The key is to flatten out and at least grab the end.

End—There is no pin, but he will have the off guard to him flat in the pull lane. The end should attack him with a far-shoulder technique. The end must not allow the play to hit inside him. He should spill the play.

Bandit—When the fullback is to but the guard is away, he goes to the POA.

Sam—When the fullback is to but the guard is away, he goes to the POA. We have had some success with fitting Sam in over the center area. There is a nice crease between the weak guard's down block and the center's turnback block on the tackle.

Will—The fullback goes away, but the guard blocks down. The only time the guard blocks down with no red motion is on the criss cross. Will must get over the top of the tackle's block. The end will spill the play to Will, who is unblocked.

Weak Corner—Plays man on #1 to late second contain.

Strong Corner—The corner's man goes away. However, we do not chase him because there may be something coming out of the front door—the criss-cross keep, for example.

Strong Safety—The safety's key goes away. The safety can play it one of two ways. He can go to the POA or he can hang along with the strong corner for the criss-cross keep.

Free Safety—When both backs go away, the safety's eyes go to the wing area. If he gets color coming back to him, he attacks for the bounce out. Another tip-off for the safety is if the weak guard blocks down. The weak guard is keyed peripherally by the safety anyway for a waggle read.

10

Attacking the Strongside Belly Series

This series attacks the defense with plays off-tackle, outside, away from flow, and play-action pass. To successfully defend the Wing-T, this series—with its ability to attack flowside via G scheme, options, and passes, combined with the ability to counter off the same action—must be stopped.

In this chapter we take the strongside belly series and show, by position, how we would play it.

G SCHEME

By position, we would play the G scheme as follows (see Diagram 10-1):

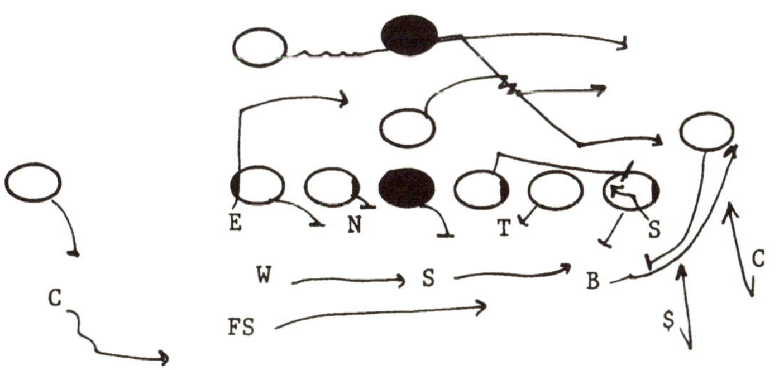

DIAGRAM 10-1
G Scheme

Tackle—When he feels the tackle's pressure, he comes backdoor or cross-faces when he is sure it is not a trap.

Nose—Penetrates and comes backdoor.

Stud—With the fullback to him, he thinks kickout or G scheme. This puts him under the guard's block. He must get his head and shoulder in the C gap, far shoulder the play, and make it spill. He cannot allow a seam inside.

End—With no pin, no pull-lane threat, and the back and QB away, the end goes to late chase.

Bandit—With the fullback and guard to, Bandit plays half a man over the top of the wing for the bounce out.

Sam—Sees the tailback on his blue motion, and the fullback will slide step. Sam takes his eyes to the wing area. If the wing is attacking the LOS, Sam plays inside out.

Will—Sees the tailback flash on his blue motion, and the fullback will slide step. Will takes his eyes to the wing area. If the wing is attacking the LOS, Will plays inside out.

Weak Corner—Plays man on #1 to cutoff.

Strong Corner—The wing may be soft or upfield as he influences the Stud. The corner must respect this as a pass release until he sees him definitely block Bandit. When he reads a block on Bandit, he will force the play and look for a spill out.

Strong Safety—Must respect pass if the tight end is soft or upfield. When he reads a block, he fills where needed.

Free Safety—When both backs are away, he eyeballs the wing area. If the wing is upfield, the safety plays B gap to fold.

BELLY DOWN OPTION

By position, we would play the belly down option as follows (see Diagram 10-2):

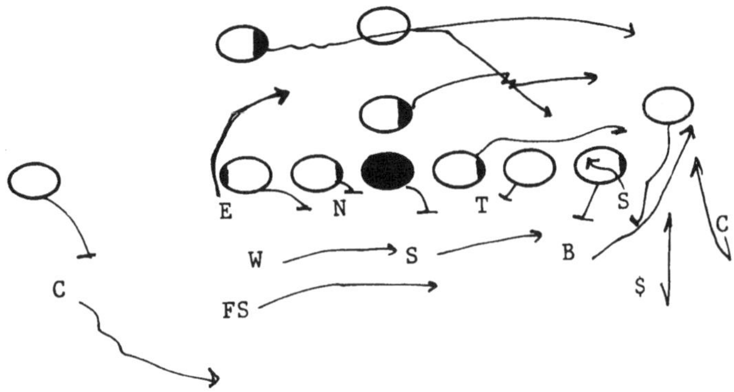

DIAGRAM 10-2
Belly Down Option

Tackle—Plays trap first. When he feels the tackle, he goes backdoor or cross-faces.

Nose—Penetrates backdoor.

Stud—When the fullback is to him, he thinks kickout or G scheme and goes under the block.

End—With no pin, no pull-lane threat, and the back and QB away, the end has late chase.

Bandit—When both the fullback and guard are to him, Bandit must get over the top of the wing's block and take the first thing that shows. In this case it will be the QB.

Sam—When the fullback flashes on his blue motion, Sam takes his eyes to the wing area. If the wing is downhill, he plays the run inside out.

Will—When the fullback flashes on his blue motion, Will takes his eyes to the wing area. If the wing is downhill, he plays the run inside out.

Weak Corner—Plays man on #1 to cutoff.

Strong Corner—Must respect the wing's upfield movement as a pass release. He will go to the pitch when he sees the wing's block on Bandit.

Strong Safety—Will fill where needed when he reads run.

Free Safety—With both backs away, he will find the tight-end/wing area. With the wing upfield, he will attack B gap to fold.

BELLY KEEP PASS

By position, we would play the belly keep pass as follows (see Diagram 10-3):

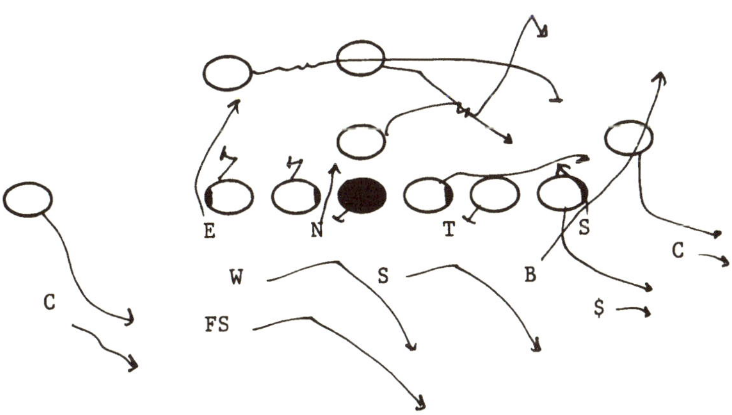

DIAGRAM 10-3
Belly Keep Pass

Tackle—Plays trap until the ball crosses his face. He cross-faces or comes backdoor.

Nose—Penetrates and comes backdoor.

Stud—The fullback will be to him. Stud will go under the fullback for the G scheme.

End—Plays contain pass rush when the tackle shows a pass block.

Bandit—With both the fullback and the guard to Bandit, he will run through. He has contain.

Sam—Will see the tailback flash on his blue motion. He then takes his eyes to the tight-end/wing area. With the tight end and wing downhill and the ball leaving the LOS, he will get depth and sling the coverage.

Will—Sees the tailback flash on his blue motion. He then takes his eyes to the tight-end/wing area. With the tight end and wing downhill and the ball leaving the LOS, he will get depth and sling the coverage.

Weak Corner—Plays man on #1.

Strong Corner—When the wing releases, the corner takes him man.

Strong Safety—Takes the tight end man to man.

Free Safety—With both backs away, he will eyeball the wing/tight-end area. When the ball leaves the LOS, he will gain depth looking for crossers.

11

Attacking the Red Motion Series

The wing motion series, with red motion, has been called the heart and soul of the offense. We welcome red motion. In many cases certain defenders can narrow their vision and key only one man.

In this chapter we take the red motion series and show, by position, how we would play it.

RED TRAP

By position, we would play the red trap as follows (see Diagram 11-1):

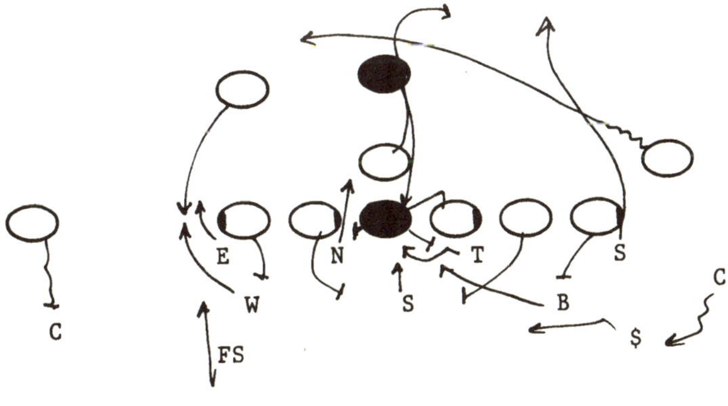

DIAGRAM 11-1
Red Trap

Tackle—Cross-faces the center's turnback block.

Nose—Penetrates. The nose will be trapped, but Sam will be unblocked at the POA.

Stud—With the "Red" call, he will eye the QB. When Stud sees the QB's face, he will be upfield. Versus the trap, he will search the QB.

End—With red motion and the tailback outside, he will be upfield.

Bandit—With red motion, Bandit keys the strong guard. When the guard pulls away, Bandit plays trap to sweep.

Sam—Versus red motion, he keys the fullback. With the fullback down the midline, Sam will tackle him. Sam will be unblocked at the POA.

Will—Versus red motion and the tailback outside, Will plays sweep.

Weak Corner—Plays man on #1 to cutoff.

Strong Corner—Gives a "Red" call, loosens, and keys the strong guard. Plays from trap to sweep to cutoff.

Strong Safety—Keys the tight end and feels the guard pull away. Plays trap to sweep.

Free Safety—With red motion, he keys the tailback. With the tailback outside, he plays him for sweep or waggle, depending on whether he blocks the end or not.

RED SWEEP

By position, we would play the red sweep as follows (see Diagram 11-2):

Tackle—Cross-faces the center's turnback block.

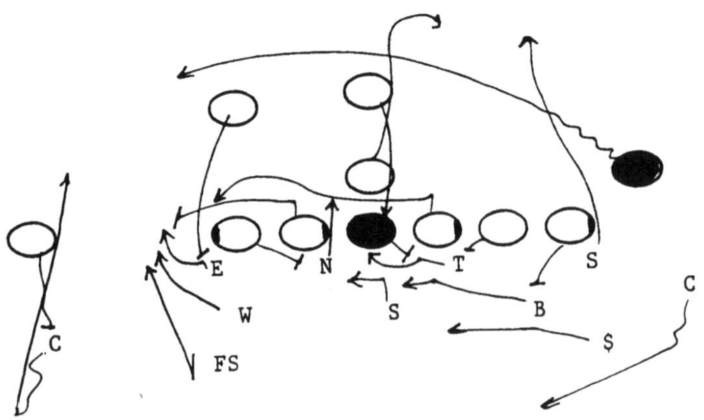

DIAGRAM 11-2
Red Sweep

Nose—Penetrates. This presents an uphill block for the tackle. The nose should at least knock off the backside guard.

Stud—Will be hard upfield when he sees the QB's face. He searches the QB.

End—The tailback will block down on him. He tight cross-faces his block.

Bandit—Plays trap to sweep.

Sam—Plays trap to sweep.

Will—Must get over the top of the tailback's block. He plays the guard down the middle.

Weak Corner—Keys the three-step drop to #1 and plays secondary support.

Strong Corner—With the guard away, he will play trap, counter, sweep to cutoff.

Strong Safety—Keys the tight end and feels the guard. With the guard away, he will play trap to sweep, B gap to fold technique.

Free Safety—The tailback will block down on the end. The free safety will force.

RED OPTION

By position, we would play the red option as follows (see Diagram 11-3):

Tackle—Closes with the guard's down block.

Nose—Penetrates.

Stud—Goes upfield to chase.

End—Tight cross-faces the tailback's down block.

Bandit—Plays backside fill to the ball off the guard's jump-through block.

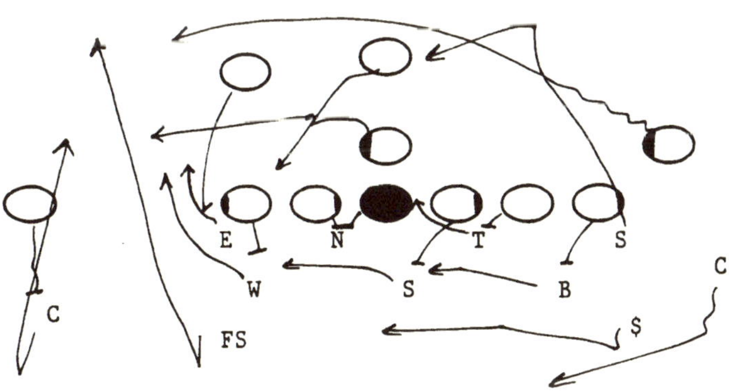

DIAGRAM 11-3
Red Option

Sam—When the fullback steps away, Sam takes his eyes to the tailback. The tailback will be downhill. Sam will scrape.

Will—When the tailback blocks down on the end, Will fits in over the top and takes the QB on the option.

Weak Corner—Keys the three-step drop to #1 and plays secondary contain.

Strong Corner—When the guard blocks down, he will play trap, counter, sweep to cutoff.

Strong Safety—When the guard blocks down, he will play trap to sweep, B gap to fold.

Free Safety—When the tailback blocks down on the end, this puts the safety on force. He will take the pitch.

RED ISOLATION

By position, we would play the red isolation as follows (see Diagram 11-4):

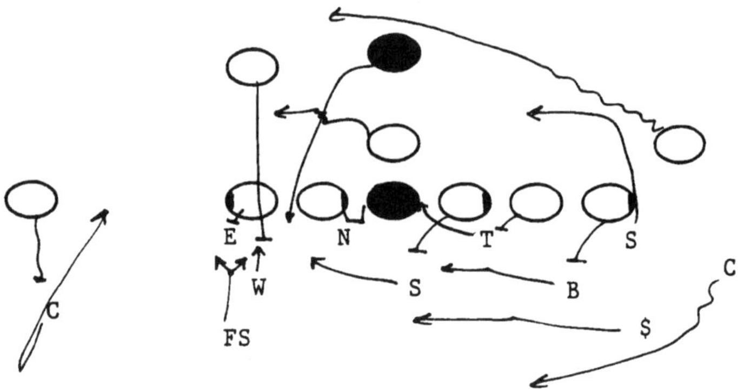

DIAGRAM 11-4
Red Isolation

Tackle—Closes off the jump-through block of the guard.

Nose—Penetrates.

Stud—Goes upfield to chase.

End—Squeezes the base block of the tackle whenever the tailback inserts inside the box. In some cases he may even cross-face the tackle's block.

Bandit—When the guard steps away, Bandit will play backside fill to inside out on the ball.

Sam—When the fullback steps away, Sam will take his focus to the tailback. If the tailback is downhill, Sam will attack inside out to the ball.

Will—Will's key will run right at the Will. If he is aligned in the cheat position, he will fold around, meet him in the hole with outside leverage, and force the ball back inside to Sam.

Weak Corner—Keys the three-step drop to #1 and plays secondary support.

Strong Corner—With the guard pulling away, the corner will think trap, counter, sweep to cutoff.

Strong Safety—With the guard pulling away, he will play B gap to fold.

Free Safety—Whenever his key leads on the Will, he will go to stack with the end. He will be able to explode outside if the ball bounces out or fall inside if the ball stays inside.

SALLY

By position, we would play the Sally as follows (see Diagram 11-5):

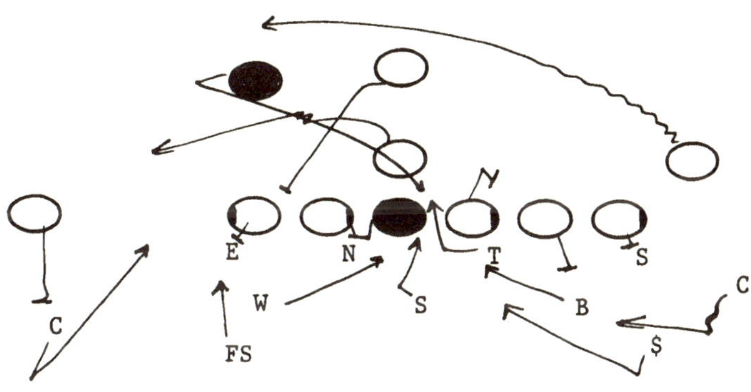

DIAGRAM 11-5
Sally

Tackle—The guard's pass set is a trap read to the tackle. He will get under the influence block. He must not overpenetrate because the ball will hit underneath.

Nose—Penetrates and splits the double team.

Stud—Squeezes the base block.

End—Squeezes the base block.

Bandit—The guard's pass set sends Bandit to his backside fill. Bandit is unblocked at the POA.

Sam—When the fullback steps away, Sam will pick up the tailback. If he counter steps, Sam will beat him to the POA.

Will—Will's key counter steps. Will should beat him to the POA.

Weak Corner—Keys the three-step drop to #1 to cutoff on runs away.

Strong Corner—With the pass set, he thinks counter to belly keep pass.

Strong Safety—With the guard's pass set, he thinks counter to belly keep pass.

Free Safety—Whenever the safety's key counter steps, the safety must think counter pass. He must feel if the fullback is leaking out on a route. If the fullback is releasing, the safety has him man. If the fullback is solid on the end, the safety falls off inside for the counter.

BELLY KEEP PASS

By position, we would play the belly keep pass as follows (see Diagram 11-6):

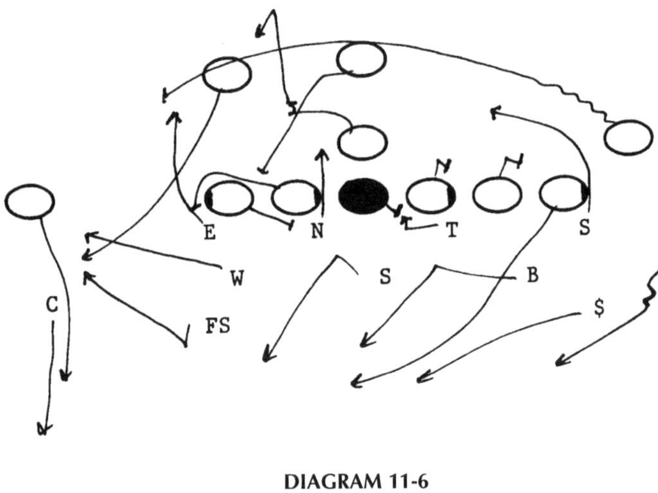

DIAGRAM 11-6
Belly Keep Pass

Tackle—Cross-faces the center's turnback block after he goes under the guard's pass set.

Nose—Penetrates and beats the tackle's block.

End—With the tailback stepping outside, this should take the end outside. He plays contain rush.

Bandit—With a pass set by the guard, Bandit thinks backside fill. When the ball leaves the LOS, he gains depth looking for crossers.

Sam—With the fullback away, Sam finds the tailback. If the tailback is on a flat route, he gains width looking for crossers.

Will—Jumps the tailback in the flat. He takes a chance and shoots the hip for the interception.

Weak Corner—Keys the three-step drop to #1 and plays man on #1.

Strong Corner—With the guard on a pass set, thinks Sally to cutoff. With the ball leaving the LOS, looks for crossers.

Strong Safety—If the tight end is on a route, the safety will take him. If the end blocks, the safety will get depth.

Free Safety—Takes the tailback in the flat. The safety will have underneath help from Will.

RED WAGGLE

By position, we would play the red waggle as follows (see Diagram 11-7):

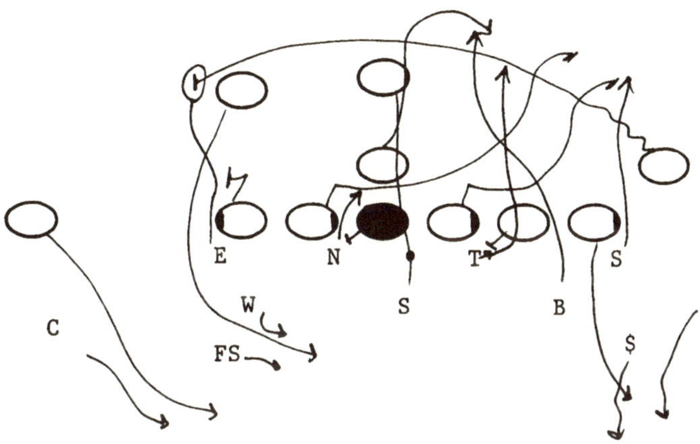

DIAGRAM 11-7
Red Waggle

Tackle—Plays trap first. When he feels pressure from the tackle, he will backdoor or cross-face to the QB.

Nose—Penetrates and backdoors the center to the QB.

Stud—With red motion, Stud takes his eyes from the fullback to the QB. If Stud sees the QB's face, he accelerates upfield. This will pull the QB up. We want to eat up both guards' blocks.

End—With red motion, the end takes his eyes to the tailback. If the tailback is on a pass release, he will run a course outside the end. The end will respect this threat to his outside shoulder. When the end feels the tailback releasing on a route, he will work upfield to the wing. The end has screen responsibility. If the wing is still motoring in this area, the end will tackle him or knock him off-course.

Bandit—With red motion, he takes his eyes from the fullback/guard key to the guard only. When the guard pulls to him, Bandit becomes a run-through player on the waggle. He finds a crack and hits it. With the QB pulled up and the Stud drawing both guards' blocks, Bandit many times will be unblocked.

Sam—Versus red motion, Sam takes his focus from his fullback/guard read to the fullback only. With the fullback down the midline, Sam will tackle him in the A gap. This is not illegal because the QB has just faked the ball to him. If we tackle him, we have eliminated a potential pass receiver. If the back takes a wider course on his route, Sam will match his angle and cover him on his flat route. The strong corner will give Sam help so Sam is not isolated on him.

Will—Versus red motion, Will takes his eyes from his fullback/guard read to the tailback. Will basically matches the tailback's angle. On the red waggle, the back will release outside. Will uses a catch technique and plays man under on the tailback with the free safety over the top.

Weak Corner—Plays man on #1.

Strong Corner—The corner will call "Red" when the wing goes into motion. The corner triggers the red scheme with his call. Versus deep red motion, the corner will loosen and widen and key the strong guard. If the guard pulls to the strong corner, he thinks waggle and will help Sam with the fullback in the flat. If Sam has eliminated the fullback, the corner continues to get depth and will play under the tight end on a corner route. If the guard pulls away from the corner, he thinks trap to sweep. If the guard pass sets, he plays the Sally. Versus flat red motion, the corner will follow the wing across the formation and take him man to man. He must give Sam a flat red call to let him know he can't help Sam with the fullback on the waggle.

Strong Safety—When the strong corner makes his "Red" call, the strong safety must echo the call. The call must get across to the free safety. The strong safety will still key the tight end and feel the strong guard. If the guard pulls to the strong safety, the defender knows it is the red waggle. The safety has the tight end man to man. The safety may get underneath help from the strong corner on the corner route, but he cannot depend on it. He must not allow the tight end to blow the top off the coverage; he must stay over the top. If the guard pulls away and the end is blocking, the safety will play from trap to sweep. The safety will basically play his normal B gap to fold technique. If the guard blocks down or pass sets, he will help on the Sally or counter.

Free Safety—With red motion, the free safety will take his focus to the tailback only. If the tailback blocks the end on the sweep or option, the free safety will support. If the tailback is inside the tackle box, the safety will go to stack position to force. If the tailback counter steps, he must be aware of the fullback in the flat on the tackle trap boot. If the fullback is blocking solidly on the end, the free safety will fall inside and help on the counter. If the tailback is upfield, he will take him man on the waggle. The Will linebacker will provide under help on the tailback. The safety must stay over the top.

12

Playing the Option

Option plays have always been an important part of the Wing-T offense. Options such as the down option, trap option, and the red option have been staples of the offense for years. However, a recent innovation has presented further problems for Wing-T defenders. Many teams have started running options that are a hybrid of Wing-T philosophies and the wishbone. We have taken our reads and keys and applied them to attacking the various options presented by the Wing-T. The defensive coach must decide how much of the offense's game plan involves the option. Is it an important ingredient in the offensive package or is it a minimal part of the package? Defensive adjustments depend upon the answers to these questions. For example, the Stud may have to change his read from the fullback to the guard.

Diagram 12-1 illustrates the triple option. By position, we would play the triple option as follows:

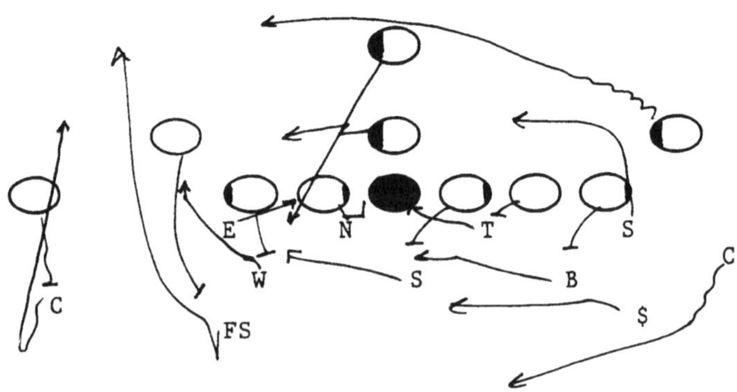

DIAGRAM 12-1
Triple Option

Tackle—Closes versus the down block. He must not allow the offensive tackle to shoeshine.

Nose—Penetrates and tries to split the double team.

Stud—The QB's back will be to the Stud. He should close, then use his chase technique.

End—This is an adjustment that must be made versus teams that run the option as an integral part of their offense. Normally versus red motion, the end would step out to the tailback on this action, but versus the option, this part of the defensive scheme obviously cannot be used. The end must close and tackle the dive.

Bandit—When the guard blocks down, the Bandit will play backside fill to inside out to the ball.

Sam—Sam's reads are the same. When the fullback goes away and the tailback is downhill, he will attack the ball inside out.

Will—Will's reads need to be adjusted. He can still key the tailback, but this key alone will not tip him off as to whether the play is the red waggle or a run. Will must vision the fullback peripherally. If the fullback is away, he will play the tailback's upfield angle as a pass and jump the tailback. If the fullback is to Will, he now knows it is the option and will scrape to the QB.

Weak Corner—Keys the three-step drop to #1 and plays secondary support.

Strong Corner—With the guard away, plays trap, sweep to cutoff.

Strong Safety—Plays B gap to fold.

Free Safety—Forces through the tailback's arc block to the pitch.

If your opponent likes to load the Will with the tailback, a good change-up is to send Will to the pitch and put the free safety on the QB. See Diagram 12-2.

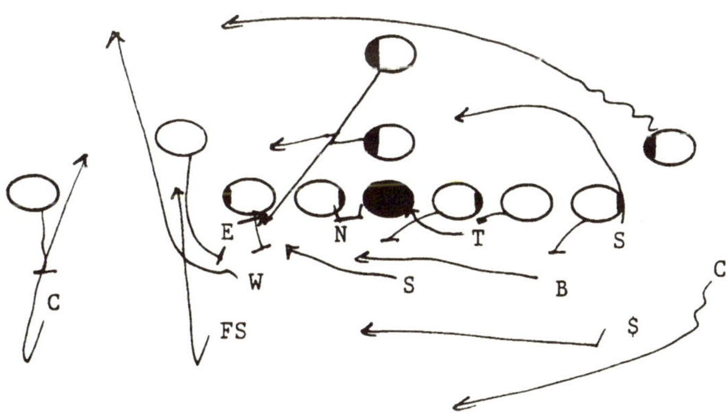

DIAGRAM 12-2
Switch

This allows the Will some operating room. This change-up also allows the free safety to sit on the dump. See Diagram 12-3.

Many teams like to go unbalanced and run the option. See Diagram 12-4.

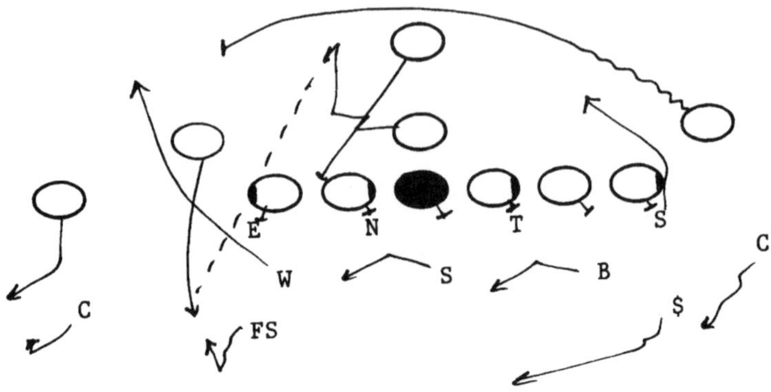

DIAGRAM 12-3
Dump

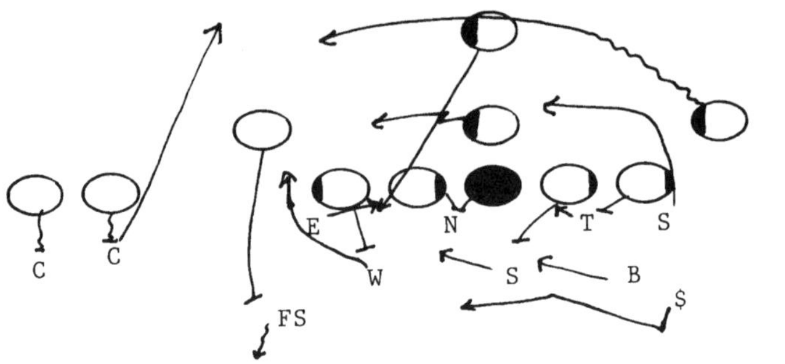

DIAGRAM 12-4
Unbalanced Option

Versus this formation, we would put Will on the QB and have the inside corner force because the inside man is covered up. This allows the safety to sit on the dump.

With the corner coming over, the unbalanced-look offenses will try to attack to the weak side.

Stud will take the dive with Bandit flying to the QB. The strong safety will take the pitch. Should the offense choose to load Bandit, we would make a "Switch" call and have Bandit take the pitch and the safety take the QB. See Diagram 12-5.

The defense must be aware that the offense can "Sally" off this same action. Our normal reads would be sufficient to take care of this play. See Diagram 12-6.

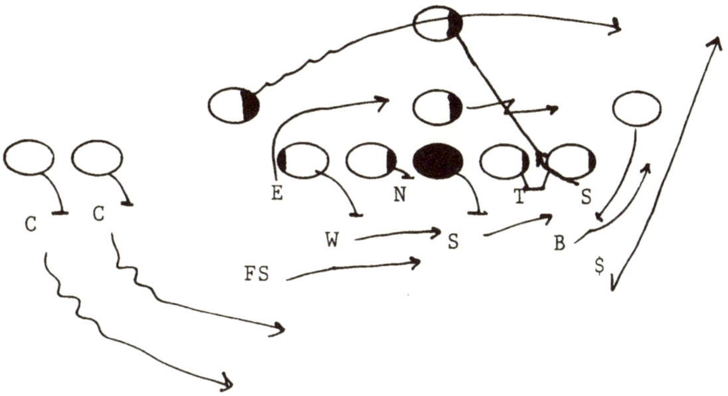

DIAGRAM 12-5
Option to Weak Side

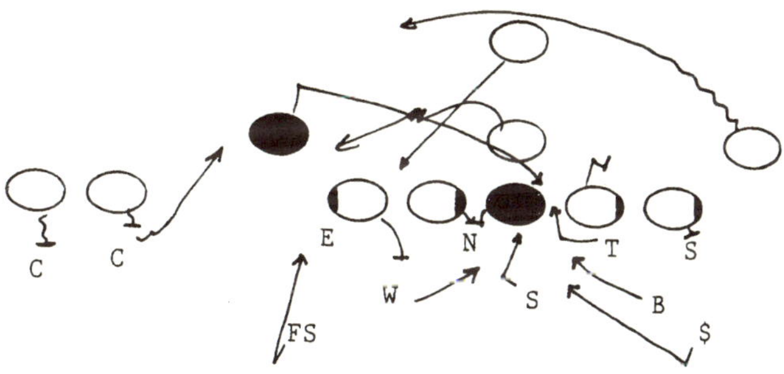

DIAGRAM 12-6
Sally

13

How to Implement the Plan

Obviously this scheme cannot be taught during the week prior to playing a Wing-T opponent. We prepare year-round to face the Wing-T. A lot of off-season time is spent on the Wing-T. During summer workouts we work on the Wing-T every other week. We have spent time on the Wing-T during fall camp even though until recently we did not face a Wing-T team until late in the schedule. The fact that we use many of our basic reads and keys versus the Wing-T helps to be prepared. We don't have to come up with an unorthodox scheme when we play the Wing-T, although we try to have a change-up or two each game.

We also don't use a lot of fronts or coverages versus the Wing-T. During practice we constantly stress "Trust your keys." We tell players that if the key takes you to the wrong place, it is the coach's fault. However, if you don't go where the key goes and your read should take you, you don't play. We demand that the players sell out on their keys. In order to feel comfortable with all the misdirection and looks the offense will show the defense, your players must be repetitioned to death during the week. The defense must be coached on the run; you should stop practice and make corrections only if there is a glaring mistake or problem. Coach the refinements between plays. Filming group and team periods is a must. This allows you to get the maximum number of reps possible and not overlook any misreads or other problems. Also, the practice film can be used as a great teaching tool during the week.

One of the practice problems defenses face when preparing for the Wing-T is that the scout offense has to be able to give a good look to the defense. In many cases the defensive staff will end up coaching the scout team on how to run the offense more so than it teaches the defense how to defend it. Coaching assignments should allow the defensive coaches to coach defense. No matter how good a job the service team does to prepare the defense, it won't be close to the game speed that the defense will see during the game. You can expect it to take awhile for the defense to adjust to the speed of play. Offensively your team cannot put the defense in duress by poor field position or turnovers early in the game.

It is a good idea to present the offense in a logical progression. If players were presented the whole offense, they would be overwhelmed. It is a must that some confidence be established. The first thing we present to the defense is the 20 series. We show how the 20 series attacks three areas with the same backfield action. We always work inside out. Start with the trap, both influence and down. Show the gut play. Next show the sweep, then the waggle. When these are understood, we move to the 30 series. We show the power sweep, then the counter criss cross. The next step in the progression is red motion with all its variations of plays—waggle, trap sweep, isolation, option, tackle trap, Sally, and belly keep pass. Last, we cover the blue motion belly series.

The practice schedule should have built in each day a short adjustment period for wheels and shifts. Normally we have a 10-minute adjustment period daily. One of the best things we do in practice is run plays without a ball. Defenders must depend upon their keys and reads because they cannot peek at the ball. We do this in a structured period, and we will occasionally script in plays in team defense where we do not use a ball. We make a big deal in practice about communication. Players are penalized when they don't initiate a call they are supposed to or when they don't echo a call such as the "Red" call. Formation recognition is a must. We insist that the formation be recognized and called by the safeties and linebackers on each play.

As most coaches know, any game is at least 90 percent mental. However, many coaches do not prepare their players psychologically to face the Wing-T. Time is spent on recognition and on the physical demands that playing the game will place on players, but not much time is spent on psychological preparation. Each player must understand his role in the game plan. The 3-technique tackle must understand that he is a trap player first and foremost. He is not expected to make every tackle or sack the QB on every pass. His job is to defeat the trap.

It is imperative the Stud understand that he will be pinned by the onside guard on the belly keep pass and the belly option, but that he will be a major factor versus the G scheme or off-tackle kickout. The Stud's thought is that he will take the G scheme out of the offensive coordinator's selection of plays. He is prepared to be pinned on the belly keep pass, but they will not run the G scheme!

Unless each player understands his role in the game plan, he can become frustrated and begin to freelance. Part of our psychological preparation is to sell each individual player on the concept that he, personally, will take the offense out of particular plays.

We tell our 3-technique tackle that the offense will have to scrap their trap game because of him. We stress to him that he, personally, will stop the trap and cause the offense to give up on the play. We convince him that the offense will have to tear that page from its playbook. This line of thinking keeps him from getting frustrated if he does not make tackles on the sweep.

We tell the nose that the offense will have to make major blocking adjustments because of his penetration on each play. The offense will have to solid block the waggle or pull the tackle instead of the guard on the red sweep. This makes it more palatable for him when he gets trapped on the red trap.

Just as defenses do when they face the option, we give each player well-defined responsibilities. Just as coaches don't ask a tackle to take the dive and QB on the same play, we don't ask a particular player to play sweep and trap on the 20 series. Each position takes pride in the fact that because of its play we have forced the offense to narrow its game plan. We will not allow the offense to attack players who have dual responsibilities. The Wing-T is famous for this concept. We ask certain players to attack given plays with the understanding that we will always have some players overlapping each play so if we get pinned or our key sends us to another area, we are still sound.

HARDING PRESS, INC.
P.O. BOX 141
HAWORTH, NJ 07641
(877) 767-7114
FAX: (201) 767-8745
hardingpress@earthlink.net
www.hardingpress.com

The following coaching books and video are available from **Harding Press.** You will find a convenient order form on the following page. If you would like information about becoming a Harding Press author, please feel free to call or write.

Thank you for your support.

Football's Explosive Multi-Bone Attack, T. DeMeo	$15.00
Coaching Run-and-Shoot Football, A. Black	$14.00
Coaching the Defensive Backfield, G. McMackin	$15.00
Eagle Five-Linebacker Defense. F. Shurmur	$15.00
Defensing the Run and Shoot, B. Kenig	$14.00
Coaching Team Defense, 2nd edition, F. Shurmur	$14.00
Coaching the Defensive Line, F. Shurmur	$16.00
Coaching the Defensive Line (video), F. Shurmur	$30.00
Football's Modern 4-3 Defense, B. Kenig	$18.00
Football's Modern Zone Blocking, J. Durham	$14.00
Stopping the Wing-T with the 4-3 Defense, B. Kenig	$15.00
Football's Matchup Zone Coverages, J. Durham	$15.00
Pro-Style Multiple Defense for High School Football, A. Black	$15.00

HARDING PRESS, INC.
P.O. BOX 141
HAWORTH, NJ 07641
(877) 767-7114
FAX: (201) 767-8745
hardingpress@earthlink.net
www.hardingpress.com

ORDER FORM

# of COPIES	TITLE	PRICE	TOTAL

Postage & Handling

SUBTOTAL ____________

Order	U.S.	Outside U.S.	
Under $25.00	$ 4.00	$ 8.25	NJ Residents
$ 25.00–$ 49.99	$ 5.50	$11.00	Add 6% Sales Tax____
$ 50.00–$ 74.99	$ 6.75	$12.25	
$ 75.00–$ 99.99	$ 8.00	$13.25	P & H ____________
$100.00–$149.99	$ 8.75	$14.00	
$150.00–$199.99	$ 9.50	$15.00	TOTAL____________
$200 +	$10.25	$15.50	

EACH ORDER MUST BE ACCOMPANIED BY CHECK, M.O., P.O., or CREDIT CARD info

COACH'S NAME ______________________________

ADDRESS ______________________________

____

CITY ______________ **STATE**________ **ZIP**________

PHONE # (___) ______________
area code

MASTERCARD/VIS ______________________________
Card # **Exp. Date**

____
Signature